UNEQUALED

JAMES A. RUNDE
WITH
DIANA GIDDON

UNEQUALED

TIPS FOR BUILDING A SUCCESSFUL CAREER THROUGH EMOTIONAL INTELLIGENCE

WILEY

Published by John Wiley & Sons, Inc., Hoboken, New Jersey.

Published simultaneously in Canada.

Library of Congress Cataloging-in-Publication Data:

Name: Runde, James A., 1946- author.
Title: UnEQualed: Tips for Building a Successful Career through Emotional Intelligence / James A. Runde.
Description: Hoboken, New Jersey : John Wiley & Sons, 2016. | Includes index.
Identifiers: LCCN 2016013558 (print) | LCCN 2016015925 (ebook) | ISBN 9781119081456 (cloth) |
ISBN 9781119246084 (ePDF) | ISBN 9781119246114 (ePub) | ISBN 9781119246084 (pdf) |
ISBN 9781119246114 (epub)
Subjects: LCSH: UnEQualed—Vocational guidance. | Financial services industry—United States.
Classification: LCC HG4534 .R86 2016 (print) | LCC HG4534 (ebook) | DDC 332.660973—dc23
LC record available at https://lccn.loc.gov/2016013558

Cover Design: Paul McCarthy

Printed in the United States of America

V10007516_011119

This book is dedicated
with love to my wife, Barbara,
who always brings out the best in me.

CONTENTS

Preface xi
Acknowledgments xv

1. Navigating Your Career (How to Manage Yourself) 1
I. What Is There Other Than Brains and Hard Work? 3
II. Emotional Quotient (EQ) 5
Adaptability 6
Adapting to Adversity 7
Collaboration 8
Empathy 9
III. The Three *D*s: Details, Deadlines, and Data 13
Details Always Matter 15
Know Your Deadlines 17
Get the Data Right! 19
IV. Expectations and Evaluations 23
Promotion Committee 24
Grab That Cup of Coffee with the Boss 26
V. Networking: Risks, Benefits, and Tips 29
Benefits of Networking 31
Be Systematic 31
Icebreakers 32
Currency 33

VI. Where Are You? 35
How to Be Happier 37
Create a Roadmap to Your Dream Job 38
Navigating the Headwinds and Tailwinds of Your Career 39
VII. Selling Yourself 41
Speak Up 42
VIII. The Path to Sponsorship 45
Role Models 45
Mentors 46
Sponsors 48
IX. Magic Formula 51
Ability 51
Opportunity 52
Courage 52

2. Becoming More Commercial (How to Work with Your Clients) 55
X. Why Is Being Commercial Relevant to You? 57
Turn Client Relationships into Revenue 58
How to Be More Commercial 59
XI. How to Win Business 63
The Art of Building Client Relationships 67
How to Monetize Client Relationships 69
How to Better Persuade Others 72
XII. How to Prepare for the Client Meeting 75
The Four *Rs* 75
Change of Mindset 78
Have a Strong Opening and Strong Close 79
How to Ask for the Order 81
Dealing with Rejection 82

XIII. Differentiating Yourself with Clients 85
Differentiating Yourself through Likability and Trust 85
Differentiating Yourself through Insight 87
Using the Apple Five Steps of Service 89
XIV. Assessing the Client Situation 91
Know Your Client's Vital Signs 91
How to Know if You Are Making Progress with a Client 92
XV. How Firm Strategy Is Commercial 95
Know Your Firm's Strategy 95
Connect Firm Strategy to Commercial Impact 96
Clients Hire Your Firm and They Hire You 97
Trust-Based Client Relationships 100

3. Becoming an Exceptional Leader 103
XVI. Engaging and Leading People 105
Three Hats 108
Three *C*s of Team Building 111
Screening Prospective Team Members 112
XVII. The War for Talent 117
The Three *M*s 119
Be Alert to the Three *D*s 121
Values and Culture 123
XVIII. Importance of Exceptional Leadership 125
Herzberg's Motivation-Hygiene Theory 125
A Team Never Forgets How You Make Them Feel 127
Importance of Optimistic Leadership 128
Definition of a Good Boss 130
Knee-Jerk Reaction 132
Adaptive Leadership 134
XIX. Control the Controllables 137

XX. Closing Advice 139

Ten Books that Might Help You 139

Highly Practical Tips 142

Summary 145

About the Author 147

Index 149

PREFACE

When a team of us worked on the United Parcel Service IPO, it was the largest IPO in history at that time. A group from Columbia Business School read about the deal in the *Wall Street Journal* and asked if I would give a speech explaining how we had won such a large piece of business. This deal was unusual because UPS chose Morgan Stanley to be the lead underwriter without talking to any other investment banks.

The speech that I made to the Columbia Business School students discussed the importance of emotional intelligence quotient (EQ), trust-based client relationships, and other soft skills. The presentation was well received, and word-of-mouth created demand at IBM, Princeton University, Davis Polk & Wardwell, and throughout Morgan Stanley. I heard the presentation was popular because I was authentic in telling stories and explaining what I had learned both from my mistakes and from the experience of others. Audiences also told me they liked hearing practical advice from a practitioner.

I had been a reader of self-help books for many years, but found most of them to be irrelevant or in the "dare to be great" genre. I also read books about finance and banking; they were full of complex equations, but many of them said nothing about "client"—not even in the index. I could not find a book that provided useful tricks of the trade for professional services people in banking, consulting, law, or accounting. I began to see that my presentation might help fill that need.

Over time, demand grew for my presentation, which resembled the first section of this book. This talk, called "Navigating Your Career," was especially popular among new hires and on business school campuses. Later, I learned that mid-level bankers were asking themselves how they could become more commercial. It was hard to find a credible outside teacher or speaker to address this issue. I was asked to create another speech based on my experience with clients. The second section of this book grew out of the commercial presentation. About five years ago, I was told that since I had helped junior bankers navigate their careers and mid-level bankers bring in more business, I should create a talk that would help senior people who were becoming managers and leaders in the firm. The third part of the book is based on working with this more senior group.

Soon I was doing as many as 50 presentations annually around the world. The presentations were unique because I focused on practical tips, I always shared my slides afterward, and I always asked for email feedback on ways to make my presentations better. Those emails often led to one-on-one coffees. Many of those coffee-mates kept in touch and asked for input as their careers progressed. My talks grew stronger because of this feedback.

This book is the compilation of those three presentations, the feedback I received from my colleagues, and the lessons I learned from those mentoring sessions. I wrote this book because I wanted to help others succeed in their professional services careers. So here it is.

That's why I wrote the book. Now who should read this book?

I have learned through giving these speeches over the years that my presentations are relevant well beyond investment banking. This book is an important guide for any person whose success is dependent on the importance of EQ and trust-based client relationships and who wants to succeed in a professional services career. This book is just as pertinent for the person who is just starting a career in professional services as it is for the seasoned professional. The first section of this book tells a junior person how to make a "job" in professional services into a "career" in professional services. The second section provides advice for anyone who is covering clients or preparing to cover clients. The third section is an important guide for anyone who is taking on a leadership role in a professional services firm, whether you are leading a small team or a large part of a professional services organization.

That's who should read this book. So why should you read it?

Banks and other professional services firms are facing a shortage of talent, especially talent with the right mindset, which means a proven ability to network, create trust-based client relationships, lead people, embrace the firm's strategy and culture, and deliver commercial results. My goal in this book is to help you to learn from my experience—and my mistakes—so that you can be the right talent with the right mindset at every stage of your career.

The critical distinguishing factor in a successful professional services career today is EQ. Emotional intelligence is the ability to monitor your own and other people's emotions, to discriminate between different emotions and label them appropriately, and to use emotional information to guide thinking and behavior. It is the single biggest predictor of performance in the workplace and the strongest driver of leadership and personal excellence. Over my 40-year career, I have learned how you can leverage EQ to create durable relationships. Without EQ, the likelihood is that you will be your firm's "best-kept secret"—not recognized, not appreciated, not promoted, and often not properly compensated.

In this book, I show you how and why EQ and soft skills are both commercial and strategic. EQ has been used to explain why people with average IQs outperformed those with the highest IQs 70 percent of the time. EQ has become part of the business vernacular, but too often it is dismissed as either simply jargon or too much in the realm of psychology. But in my judgment, EQ is more than charisma or personality. It is exhibited in adaptability, collegiality, and empathy.

Early in your career, you will quickly discover that you, like all your colleagues, are smart and hard working. Interpersonal skills are vital to distinguishing yourself at the beginning of your career. Understanding your firm's culture and incorporating it into your behavior are other keys to getting ahead. Other important considerations at the beginning of your professional services career include communicating with your boss, networking, and finding mentors and sponsors. All of these form the foundation for what I call the magic formula of ability, opportunity, and courage.

When serving clients in the second phase of your career, trust and likeability are more powerful than having encyclopedic knowledge or knowing complex equations. It is important but difficult to build relationships and turn those relationships into revenue. You will need to master the arts of creating insight out of information and using your time wisely.

The third career phase involves leading people and building teams. This book provides evidence and examples of how to better engage and motivate knowledge workers. It explains what makes a good boss and a great leader. In today's business world, a leader needs to both anticipate and adapt to changes in technology, demographics, and volatility.

The measure of this book's success will be how well it changes your mindset and, more importantly, your behavior. My goal is to give you useful tools that will help you build a satisfying and successful career.

ACKNOWLEDGMENTS

This book reflects the impact of many people throughout my life and career. First, my parents had a powerful and positive influence on my life. My mom and dad instilled in me a deep respect for faith, education, and teamwork. I will forever be grateful for their guidance and sacrifice.

I also would like to thank the people who contributed to my career success, who taught me the ropes and showed me how to do first-class business in a first-class way. Their contributions to my professional progress were noteworthy and invaluable. Parker Gilbert was my model of integrity and financial judgment and a very loyal friend. Griff Sexton was the first person I met at Morgan Stanley and was my mentor throughout my career.

Special thanks to Morgan Stanley Chairman and CEO James Gorman and President Colm Kelleher. Both have shown themselves to be exemplary leaders of the firm through the exceedingly difficult transition period in the wake of the financial crisis. Their relentless focus on strategy, shareholder value, and cost has allowed Morgan Stanley to reshape its business model while maintaining a premiere client franchise in the investment banking industry.

This book would not have been possible without the support and encouragement of my wife, Barbara, and my children, Dan, Kevin, and Kate. As a seasoned publishing industry expert, Kate and her insights were especially valuable throughout the process.

Credit is most definitely due to the person who did so much to make this book come to life: Diana Giddon. Words cannot express my appreciation for her professional advice and her persistence and assistance in editing and polishing the manuscript. She knows the subject matter very well, as she is a consultant to professional services firms and a former investment banker.

Several individuals read the entire manuscript and offered their thoughtful comments on it. Cory Spencer not only offered helpful comments on the manuscript but was instrumental in suggesting the format and creating the basic outline. Others who earned my appreciation are my sister, Kate Raab, Lenore Pott, Ken Pott, Bob Hallinan, Peg Sullivan, Mary Clare Delaney, Jennifer Zimmerman, Rebecca Tyson, Erika Gruppo, David Darst, Daisy Dowling, Emily Rosenfield Magid, Lauren Garcia Belmonte, Felicity Tan, Ching-Ching Chen, Levi Malik, Vanessa Capodanno, Sarah Philips, Jessica Zoob, and Alison Kittrell.

The team from John Wiley & Sons has been outstanding from start to finish. Pamela van Giessen, Bill Falloon, Meg Freeborn, and Laura Gachko were essential in creating and polishing this book and all of them have my respect and gratitude.

1

NAVIGATING YOUR CAREER (HOW TO MANAGE YOURSELF)

I

WHAT IS THERE OTHER THAN BRAINS AND HARD WORK?

Have you ever wondered if you are your firm's best-kept secret? Do you wonder if brains and hard work are enough for you to succeed and get ahead at your firm?

When I started as an investment banker in 1974, I believed that brains and hard work were what got me a position at Morgan Stanley. On the first day of work, it took me about 10 minutes to realize that the woman to my right was smarter than I was and the man to my left was working harder than I was. I thought, "Oh no—there is no way I am smarter than that woman, and I can't work at that guy's pace. I might be toast."

I concluded that there must be something else to distinguish beyond the brains and hard work that got me (and everyone else) the job. The emotional intelligence quotient, or EQ, card was the only and the best that I could play.

I learned about EQ both by being part of a big family and by working with really bright people in the Navy. I grew up in a family of 10 children in

Sparta, Wisconsin. I quickly learned how to listen. I became adaptable by relating to my siblings, who were different ages and had different interests. My parents were schoolteachers as young adults. They each taught eight grades in one-room country schoolhouses in rural Wisconsin. My parents taught us to work as a team to get things done in our home.

After graduating from Marquette University, I joined the U.S. Navy and served as an officer for five years on the nuclear energy staff of Admiral Rickover.

My first month in the Navy was very similar to my first month at Morgan Stanley. I realized that to survive and thrive, I needed more than brain power alone. By being friendly, asking and offering to help others, and creating a network, I was able to solve problems more quickly and put issues in perspective. This same approach proved effective later as I started in a professional services firm.

Early in my career, I saw how EQ (or the lack of it) was more powerful than IQ. For example, we had been trying hard to win a mergers-and-acquisitions (M&A) mandate from the Walt Disney Company. After a number of attempts, we finally persuaded the CEO of Disney to visit Morgan Stanley's New York headquarters. The head of our mergers-and-acquisitions division said we should put our most brilliant M&A banker in charge of the meeting—let's call him Bill.

Bill ordered up reams of analyses and created a huge presentation of M&A ideas, giving the CEO his best ideas. The CEO disliked all of Bill's ideas and said that he had his own pet acquisition idea, which he had not discussed with any other bankers. After the CEO told Bill his specific target and plan, Bill looked at the CEO with a straight face and asked, "Now why would you do a Mickey Mouse thing like that?"

The CEO turned red in the face, stood up, and left our building. Anyone with an ounce of EQ would have known better than to make a sarcastic remark about the icon of the potential client's company. Bill might have been very good at analyzing acquisitions, but he was a total dunce when it came to EQ.

II

EMOTIONAL QUOTIENT (EQ)

Why do people with average IQs outperform those with the highest IQs? In his book, *Emotional Intelligence: Why It Can Matter More Than IQ*, Dr. Daniel Goleman, an expert on brain and behavioral sciences, addresses emotional quotient (EQ) versus IQ.[1] EQ provides the evidence that being smart is not just a matter of mastering facts or equations; it requires mastering your own emotions and understanding the emotions of the people around you. EQ is a better predictor of success, quality of relationships, and overall happiness.

EQ is about your relationships:

- Your relationship with yourself (self-awareness/adaptability)
- Your relationships with your colleagues (collegiality/collaboration)
- Your relationships with your clients (empathy)

[1]Daniel Goleman, *Emotional Intelligence: Why It Can Matter More Than IQ* (New York, Bantam Dell, 2006) (originally published in 1995).

I think of EQ in terms of adaptability, collegiality/collaboration, and empathy, or ACE.

ADAPTABILITY

> "It is not the strongest of the species that survives, nor the most intelligent that survives. It is the one that is most adaptable to change."
>
> *Attributed to Charles Darwin, English naturalist and geologist*

Let's start with *adaptability*. There is constant change in professional services firms. Competition changes; just ask those who were once at Lehman Brothers, Bear Stearns, or Arthur Andersen. Technology changes; when I started at Morgan Stanley, there was one computer that used punch-cards for data entry. Leadership changes; Wall Street firms periodically reorganize. Regulations are replaced; for example, Dodd-Frank and the Volcker Rule have caused important strategic and structural adjustments. As a result of all these changes, adaptability is critical to success in professional services.

Your ability to adapt begins with the awareness of where you are and that you will need to change at certain points in your career. Self-awareness is your ability to recognize your emotions and how they affect your thoughts and behavior, as well as understanding your strengths and weaknesses. Self-awareness can help you to adapt to the array of different bosses with different working styles you will encounter throughout your career.

You inevitably will work on different types of projects or different types of products. You will work with an array of different clients with different personalities. For example, when a new CFO joins a client, the incumbent bankers are guilty until proven innocent. This means that the incumbent bankers need to prove themselves to the new CFO. If you are one of those incumbents, you will need to be aware of how the new CFO perceives you and be able to adapt to the new CFO and a potentially new finance team.

As you move up the corporate ladder, you will need to adapt to different roles and responsibilities. What made you a great associate will not make you a great vice president. It is hard to be on the road covering your clients as a vice president while still trying to do your own spreadsheets or research like an associate.

Almost invariably, if you look at the job specifications or performance evaluation form for vice president, you will find that what got you the promotion is not enough to get you to the next level. In *What Got You Here Won't Get You There,* author Marshall Goldsmith explains that your success and accomplishments to this point will not get you where you want to go.[2] You have to adapt in order to continue advancing your career.

ADAPTING TO ADVERSITY

"There is no education like adversity."

Benjamin Disraeli, British politician and writer

Ben Franklin is famous for his wisdom and knowledge. He said that there is nothing certain except death and taxes. I agree, but he forgot to include *adversity*. Everyone has personal and professional setbacks. I have seen co-workers have emotional outbursts or become almost catatonic when they missed a promotion, lost a deal, or were dealt some other negative surprise. In some cases, they spent so long in their funk that it damaged their career or reputation.

According to the American Psychological Association, resilience is your capacity to deal with stress, adversity, and uncertainty. Resilience is about bouncing back, rolling with the punches, or at least acting as if you have absorbed the issue and are moving ahead. Resilience can help you feel or look as if you are in control. With the proper perspective, you can deal with uncertainty or disappointment as a professional rather than acting like a victim.

Developing a mindset of optimism and making persistence a habit also improves your ability to deal with setbacks.

---

[2]Marshall Goldsmith and Mark Reiter, *What Got You Here Won't Get You There* (New York: Hyperion, 2007).

My experience has taught me that resilience can be developed and strengthened if we make it a priority. Having a strong network of positive relationships is a vital foundation for resilience. Positive social support is associated with better performance and well-being, particularly in times of stress. Do not wait until there is a crisis, but start now to methodically extend your circle of positive relationships. The people around us can have a significant impact on how we handle challenges.

Your ability to adapt to adversity is also influenced by what you do to stay in shape—physically, emotionally, and spiritually. Proper exercise, sleep, and lifestyle will make you more resilient and able to release stress when it occurs. You can't predict upsets, but you can be prepared for them so you can adapt and bounce back rather than overreact.

COLLABORATION

> "Individual commitment to group effort—that is what makes a team work, a company work, a society work, a civilization work."
>
> *Vince Lombardi, Hall of Fame football coach*

Did your kindergarten teacher ever praise you by saying that you "work and play well with others?" Through *collaboration*, a team can achieve better results than any individual could have achieved alone.

Collaboration is essential in professional services firms because the work is done primarily in an environment in which a team is united in a common purpose and team members respect each other's abilities and perspectives.

James Surowiecki's book, *The Wisdom of Crowds*, offers the simple idea that groups of people are smarter than an elite few, no matter how intelligent, innovative, or clever at problem solving the few are.[3] Surowiecki compares the traditional method of decision making by a small group of experts with the method of organizing a large group of ordinary people. He found that ordinary people can avoid the weaknesses of the expert group and thus make better decisions and predictions. He highlights the

[3]James Surowiecki, *The Wisdom of Crowds* (New York: Anchor Books, 2005).

weaknesses of traditional decision making, in which specialized experts in small, deliberative groups are assumed to be better able to make effective decisions.

The world of professional services is only becoming more collaborative. Teams are global and diverse. The workplace is virtual. There are larger teams collaborating to solve increasingly complex client problems. Often, these teams bring together expertise across products or across industries. We frequently rely more heavily on support from corporate functions like finance, internal legal, marketing, and so on. In the past, you might see a smaller deal team of bankers and one or two internal lawyers. With today's complex deal structures, it is very common for a deal team to include one or two people from up to eight different groups within a firm, like accounting, foreign exchange, commodities, technology, legal, and corporate communications.

In order to succeed in a professional services firm today, you need to work well with your colleagues so that the entire team succeeds.

EMPATHY

> "If you can learn a simple trick, Scout, you'll get along a lot better with all kinds of folks. You never really understand a person until you consider things from his point of view, until you climb inside his skin and walk around in it."
>
> *Atticus Finch in* To Kill a Mockingbird *(1962)*

Empathy is understanding what others are feeling because you have experienced it yourself or can put yourself in their shoes. Empathy allows you to build trust with your clients.

People starting out their careers in professional services think that figuring out the answer is the hard part of the job. In professional services, we are all in the solutions business, but finding the right solution is often not the difficult task. Experience has taught me that if a client tells me the problem, we have enough smart people working in a collaborative environment that we will always come up with a thoughtful response. The real challenge is getting the client to tell you the problem.

If I missed a piece of business for a client, it was not because the client did not know me or I was not smart enough. I missed the business because the client never gave me a shot at answering the question. Either the client did not think of calling me or did not trust me enough to share what was on his or her mind. The key to winning business is getting the client to trust or like you enough so they will tell you the issue on their mind.

Building a relationship of trust and openness can take years, but it pays dividends. I worked with one client for years on a mergers-and-acquisitions concept that never materialized. But over that time, I gained the client's trust because I listened and was reliable. That client ultimately awarded our firm with the lead underwriting role in the largest initial public offering in history at that time.

How do you build client trust? You need to put yourself in the other person's shoes so that you can understand and respect that person's perspectives. You can build trust only when you can communicate emotion and understanding. You develop empathy with clients by asking open-ended questions and listening to the answers. As the Greek philosopher Epictetus said, "We have two ears and one mouth so that we can listen twice as much as we speak." Only when you and the client click on a personal level and the client likes you can you build real trust.

Some professional services people think that when a client is passed over for promotion, it is best to leave the client alone and not to reach out. I have experienced the pain of being passed over for promotion. When I was passed over, I felt like I was alone. Everyone seemed to be avoiding me just at the time when I was yearning for moral support.

Remembering that painful experience, I always call a client who has had a setback. I simply tell the client that I read about the promotion decision and then I ask how I can help. It is important to have a candid conversation with the client in times of adversity—it helps to build trust.

For example, when the treasurer of a client was not picked to be the new CFO, I immediately called and told the treasurer that I thought that he or she had many professional options. I offered to give the treasurer a professional reference and make introductions to other people in his or her industry. I used that same approach many times with clients, and every time I did so, my relationship with the person soared. Everyone piles on to offer congratulations for a promotion, but few people think to offer assistance in times of adversity.

By putting yourself in your client's shoes, you show that you have empathy. This helps to build trust. That client will not forget that you were the one banker who called when he or she had a setback.

But listening alone is not enough to build client trust. You need to build your credibility with the client by showing that you have integrity and that you are reliable. In order to build integrity, your actions need to match your words. The client needs to see that you are trustworthy over time.

Empathy is important, but it is not enough on its own. In professional services, your goal is to evolve your role in client relationships from a service provider to a trusted adviser. Client trust can make or break your ability to win business. Nearly all of the deals that I won during my career were because the client trusted and liked me rather than because I had a brilliant insight or analysis.

It is important to note that empathy is not the same as sympathy. Empathy is the ability to experience the feelings of another person. It goes beyond sympathy, which is acknowledging another person's emotional hardships and providing comfort and assurance. Empathy can forge a deeper and more meaningful connection, thus serving as a bridge for greater communication between individuals or between leader and followers. Everyone should cultivate the virtue of empathy just to be a worthwhile person above and beyond the commercial value of having empathy.

III

THE THREE *Ds*: DETAILS, DEADLINES, AND DATA

> "The longer I live, the more I realize the impact of attitude on life. Attitude to me is more important than facts. . . . We cannot change our past . . . we cannot change the fact that people will act in a certain way. We cannot change the inevitable. The only thing we can do is play the one string we have, and that is our attitude. I am convinced that life is 10 percent what happens to me and 90 percent how I react to it. And so it is with you . . . we are in charge of our attitudes."
>
> *Charles R. Swindoll, theologian, author, and educator*

Especially when you are just starting out, you can impress both your bosses and your colleagues by demonstrating that you have a positive attitude and are willing to go the extra mile, for both your firm and your clients.

When I started out in investment banking, sometimes I came across to other people as unhappy. Maybe I had a sour face or I complained and acted like I was too good for certain assignments. I quickly learned that complaining and acting like you are above the work will hold you back. Don't do it!

Luckily, someone more senior took me aside to talk to me about my entitled attitude. Her basic message was, "While we were working together, I got the sense that you were unhappy with your assignments and felt you should have been given more challenging work. I was surprised when you complained about things like X, Y, and Z. You did a fine job, but these soft skills really matter, and they can even trump your work quality. I want to see you do well, and I think this might be an area for you to approach differently." I liked that someone took the time to coach me.

Having a positive attitude also can help you avoid mistakes. When you make slip-ups early in your career, they can either be stupid mistakes or careless errors. If they are stupid mistakes, then you can address those errors through training. We all make mistakes.

But if you make missteps because you do not care about your work product, that is a bigger issue because you are not "all in" or you do not have a positive attitude. It is much better to be all in with a positive attitude and make stupid mistakes that can be corrected through training.

Also early in your career, it is important to maintain perspective about the bigger picture of your career development. You do not want to be so bogged down in minutiae that you miss opportunities that will advance your career. If you have a positive attitude and are willing to do tasks that others will not do, then you will gain opportunities to learn new things, get exposure to new people, and create a professional identity as the kind of person who gets things done. Later in your career, you will have opportunities that others will not because they have not had your experiences, do not know the number of people you know, or do not have your reputation.

For example, I remember when I had been passed over for promotion the year before. The following year was really important for me, and I was laser focused on delivering revenues in order to get promoted. I was asked by two senior leaders of our firm to go to Los Angeles for the July 4th weekend to work on the firm's strategic plan. I did not have a great attitude when I was asked to give up my July 4th weekend for administrative work. I knew that I needed to bring in revenue in order to get promoted that year, and I did not see the benefit of going to Los Angeles over a holiday weekend. One of the two senior leaders assured me, though: "This is a positive thing for you to do, trust me." I went to Los Angeles with the senior leaders and maintained a positive attitude throughout the trip.

As a result of going on this trip, I developed a relationship with a senior person I would not otherwise have gotten to know. You probably will not be surprised to find out that that person played a critical role in getting me promoted later that year. I learned a lot more about our businesses and gained new perspective about the future strategic direction of our firm. Agreeing to work on the firm's future strategy and getting the details right really helped my career flourish.

When I give talks to large groups, I am frequently asked if I have any advice for someone just starting out in a professional services firm. I always tell people to pay attention to the three *Ds*—details, deadlines, and data. Let's start with the details.

DETAILS ALWAYS MATTER

Getting the details right involves two qualities or attitudes: thoroughness and resourcefulness. Although details involve the kind of work that might not be exciting, every professional services firm cares about getting them right. No matter how small the task, you should think through all of the necessary steps for a successful outcome. The best employees are strong at planning, but they are awesome at execution. In a professional services firm, getting it right the first time, having a positive attitude, and showing attention to detail greatly enhance your brand and reputation in the early days of your career.

When beginning a task, always think about how what you are doing can make your boss look better. For example, if you are in charge of planning a meeting, your goal is to create an environment where your client feels welcome and comfortable, and your boss looks organized and efficient. Make sure that you have booked the meeting room and arranged for the building security passes for the clients. Order catering ahead of time, and have the food in the meeting room before the client arrives. It is disruptive to a client meeting when caterers arrive in the middle of a meeting and people need to talk over the noise of setting up the food.

Check all technology before the client arrives. If possible, ask a technology representative to help you check your slides in the meeting room. Slides might look different depending on the computer in the meeting room. Make sure that the dial-in number for the conference call is working properly before the client arrives, especially if there are parties calling in from other locations. The details matter, and you need to prove that you can effectively manage the details before you are given greater responsibility.

If you are working through the details and you hit a roadblock, you will never find a solution without resourcefulness. Resourcefulness is the ability to quickly and cleverly find ways to overcome difficulties and solve problems. In professional services, you frequently find yourself with limited resources or time and the need to quickly solve a problem.

One way to be resourceful is to develop a good relationship with your boss's assistant. The assistant typically knows how your boss would like things done. When you show that you are a team player, your boss's assistant probably will tell the boss how much he or she enjoys working with you. The assistant's opinion can hold a lot of weight.

The boss's assistant also can help you to gain access to the boss in important situations. For example, the assistant usually is the keeper of the boss's calendar. If you are authentically nice to assistants and have a strong relationship with them, you will be amazed at how helpful they can be.

Once I was running a group in investment banking that worked closely with a banker from another part of the firm who was very important to our franchise and who really wanted to make partner. If he did not get promoted to partner, he planned to quit and go to another firm. I needed to get an appointment with the head of Investment Banking to make the case to promote our colleague.

I had a solid relationship with the assistant to the head of Investment Banking, but I could not get time on the head's schedule before the promotion committee meetings. I knew that he lived in Greenwich, Connecticut, so I asked his assistant how the boss got home from work and learned that he had a driver. The assistant was willing to let me share the boss's car home to Greenwich that night so that I could make my case face to face as we rode in the car together. It took about four minutes to have the conversation about our banking colleague's promotion. Without my strong relationship with the assistant and my resourcefulness, I would not have had the chance to help my teammate get promoted.

KNOW YOUR DEADLINES

"Experience is the name everyone gives to their mistakes."

Oscar Wilde, Irish playwright, novelist, and poet,
Lady Windermere's Fan, 1892, Act III

When I was just starting out in my business career, I learned the hard way that you need to know your deadlines. When you are a junior person, it can be really awkward to ask your boss, "When would you like to see this?" Senior people are not always clear about deadlines, so junior people need to understand their boss's expectations and deadlines. It can be challenging to manage multiple deliverables when you are overcommitted and you want to succeed on several projects at once.

On a Tuesday afternoon after I first started working at Morgan Stanley, a partner asked me to complete a task. I was intimidated by the partner. I assumed that the task was due in a few days and that it was too pushy to ask about the due date.

On Wednesday afternoon, the partner asked where the deliverables were in front of several other junior bankers. I had just started the work and was completely embarrassed in front of my new colleagues. At the time, I did not know the meaning of the word *alacrity*. The partner said to me,

"Runde, next time I ask you to do something I would like to see more alacrity." You better believe that I figured out the meaning of the word *alacrity* pretty quickly. (For those of you who may not be familiar with the word, it means "a quick and cheerful readiness to do something."[1])

It is important to ask a senior person when he or she needs an assignment completed so that you can avoid the business version of a baseball play at the plate—when the ball and the runner reach home plate at the same time. There is nothing more exciting than a play at the plate in a baseball game, but it can be disastrous in the office. If I need to leave for the airport promptly at 3 p.m., then I want the presentations in my hands at 2:55 p.m. so that I can leave for the airport on time. If I get the presentations at 3:05 p.m., then my heart rate begins to race and I lose confidence in the team.

Always set realistic expectations about deliverables. If your boss needs something in a week, do not trap yourself into a Friday night deadline; your boss probably will not look at it over the weekend. Instead, tell the boss that you will deliver the work on Monday morning. That way you have the entire weekend to work on the project and to get it in sound shape before Monday morning.

Even better, consider whether it makes sense to prepare a first draft. Then deliver the preliminary work to your boss ahead of the deadline on Thursday afternoon or Friday morning. You will have beaten your own Monday timeline. You can confirm that you understood the request and get an initial reaction to your work. In addition, you will have extra time over the weekend to make any necessary refinements. You will be on the road to building your credibility and a solid reputation.

Managing multiple projects with overlapping deliverables can also be challenging. Typically, this situation occurs when you are asked to work on a new project and you are already overcommitted on other projects. Sometimes it seems hard to resist taking on an additional project when the new assignment is presented as a chance to go with a senior banker to meet with the CEO of a client.

---

[1] *Merriam-Webster's Collegiate Dictionary*, 11th Edition.

I have seen junior people try to power through all of the projects on their plate at once. Usually, this involves taking on too much work and not sleeping to try to meet all of the deadlines. As a result of the lack of sleep, the junior person can drop a ball or make a big mistake. Pushing back on a request from your boss can be intimidating, but it is significantly better than setting yourself up to fail and disappointing your boss or the client.

One effective technique is to push back diplomatically by asking your boss to help you prioritize your project list. Specifically, you should say to your boss, "I would love to work on Project X. I am highly confident that I could do a great job, but I am already working on Projects A, B, and C. Project A is due tomorrow. Project B is a huge amount of work. The timeline for Project C has just been accelerated."

This approach allows you to have a conversation with your boss about everything that is on your plate. You are giving your boss the opportunity to prioritize the projects that are most important and perhaps delay other projects. The most important thing is to have the courage to have the prioritization discussion as soon as you are asked to work on Project X rather than accepting it, realizing you have too much work, and then asking for more time just before Project X is due. Learn from my experience.

GET THE DATA RIGHT!

And now we've reached the third and final *D*: data. Every investment bank, law firm, consulting firm, and accounting firm is hyperfocused on the quality and accuracy of data. A professional services firm builds its reputation on delivering solid analytics and accurate work product.

When I was a junior banker, there was no such thing as spellcheck. I prepared a three-page memo for a client based on a lot of rigorous analysis. I was highly confident in my work. After I finished, I brought the memo to my boss for his review before I sent it to the client. My boss immediately pointed to a misspelled word in the memo and said to me, "If there is a typo, then I am worried that there is a *thinko*." My boss, Donald, was a Yale graduate and the former editor of the *Yale Daily*. Clearly, he knew that there was no such word as *thinko*. But I got his point immediately: If the data are sloppy or the narrative is sloppy, then the client might wonder if the analysis or the judgment is also flawed.

Today there is spellcheck, so use it. But don't rely on it. Spellcheck doesn't know the difference between *from* and *form*. Consider asking someone to proofread a presentation. Then check the numbers and analytics—twice.

Several years ago while on a trip to London, I ended up on a British Airways plane across the aisle from the then-CEO of Morgan Stanley. I saw that he was reading the airline magazine during the flight. He suddenly took out his pen and circled a typo in the magazine. Then he turned to me and said, "Everyone has to pay attention to detail." I was struck by how he expected the same level of excellence from the airline publication as he would expect from any work that he saw produced by Morgan Stanley.

In the professional services business, your reputation for getting it right is critical for your career advancement. So always check your work, especially if it is going directly to the client. Re-read your email, and check the spelling before you send it. Review your presentations for poor grammar, inconsistent fonts, or typos.

Double-check your quantitative analysis. Be careful when you are copying and pasting; don't inadvertently put Client X's name on a document that was prepared for Client Y. Ask a team member or someone in your network to review your work, and offer to review their work in exchange. When you make careless mistakes, you can harm your reputation, waste your colleagues' time, and potentially cost your firm money.

There is another trap that I want you to avoid with respect to data. Resist the temptation to provide a quick answer to questions about data when you can take a few minutes to confirm that you have the right answer. For example, this situation can occur after you have done an excellent financial analysis, but time has passed and you have moved on to other assignments. Then the senior person unexpectedly asks about the old financial analysis, "Was the rate of return that you calculated for me three weeks ago pretax or after-tax?"

You are a smart and competent professional. You do not want to look as if you do not know your own financial analysis. Therefore, there is a powerful tendency to guess whether the financial analysis was pretax or after-tax rather than saying, "I don't know." I urge you not to guess.

It is much more professional to say, "I will take a look at the data and come back to you with that answer right away. Would you like me to send you an email or stop by your office?" In 40 years on Wall Street, I have never seen a question that could not wait an extra 10 minutes to check the data for accuracy.

Mastering details, deadlines, and data is a matter of having a positive attitude that prioritizes quality work and communication.

IV

EXPECTATIONS AND EVALUATIONS

Do you know the performance evaluation criteria for your current role? Most professional services firms publish the performance evaluation criteria by level. If not, you can get the performance evaluation criteria by asking human resources. These criteria are not the same as the job description; they are the scorecard that management and human resources use to grade employees. Knowing the performance evaluation criteria is like having an open-book final exam: You have all the questions in front of you. You can use the questions as a checklist to help you develop examples of how you have achieved what is asked of you at your level.

If it is a promotion year for you, you want to know the performance evaluation criteria for your current level, the level to which you hope to be promoted, and your expected behavior from your manager. Your best case for promotion is to be already functioning at the level above your current level. I have participated in thousands of promotion decisions over my career. When the conversation starts with broad agreement that Jane has been functioning at the next level for a while, then Jane is highly likely to get that promotion.

PROMOTION COMMITTEE

Why am I so confident that my advice will help you? In the promotion decisions I have been involved with, rarely was someone turned down for a promotion because he or she was not smart enough.

Professional services firms already filter for IQ in the recruiting process. When interviewing candidates, I always look for an indicator of hard work, such as summer jobs, and an indicator of brains, such as intellectual curiosity. It is also rare for someone to be turned down for a promotion because he or she did not work hard.

Professional services firms already know that you are capable of hard work because you proved yourself through your grades at school. You would not have excelled at the great school that you went to if you did not have brains and hard work.

So how are promotion decisions made when there are lots of smart people, lots of hard workers, and lots of people taking initiative on both your team and your competitors' teams?

Most problems, crises, and defeats in professional services can be traced back to issues with poor communication, teamwork, and trust, and/or an inability to persuade people that your position is correct. Most victories and achievements in professional services result from first-rate communication, teamwork, trust, and the ability to persuade. So these become the criteria that distinguish the winners in the promotion committee discussions.

I have often seen the following factors be decisive in promotion discussions:

- *Judgment:* Having an opinion and consistently making sound decisions are highly valued.
- *Arrogance:* Thinking you are better, smarter, or more important than other people is a negative factor.
- *Inclusiveness:* Reaching out to colleagues to get their input and opinions rather than consciously excluding colleagues is desirable.

- *Team player versus lone wolf:* A team beats an individual every time in this business.
- *Ethics:* Not adhering to high standards and ethics with clients is fatal in a promotion committee discussion.
- *Communication:* Having the ability to communicate internally with colleagues and externally with clients is important.
- *Long-term good of the firm:* Promotion committees look for people who are more interested in the long-term interests of the firm than in their personal compensation.
- *Encyclopedia versus trusted adviser:* The encyclopedia knows more about the client's business and competitors than about the client and spends the whole meeting talking rather than listening. Being effective with clients is about much more than mastering facts; it is about building trust with the client so that the client tells you the problem.
- *Leadership:* The potential to lead a professional services team is important.
- *Commercial instinct:* This is a critical and intangible ingredient in revenue generation that is highly valued.
- *Resilience:* Successful promotion candidates have the character, optimism, and persistence to recover from a setback.
- *Treatment of junior people:* Do you see the junior people as just an engine room, or as the next generation of talent?

My father-in-law used to say disdainfully that a person who was too bookish or academic "spent too much time in libraries and not enough time in saloons." His point was that people smarts or interpersonal skills almost always trump book smarts. The people who get promoted in professional services firms typically have the same people smarts or interpersonal skills that my father-in-law valued.

GRAB THAT CUP OF COFFEE WITH THE BOSS

A periodic cup of coffee with your boss is a good practice because it ensures your priorities match your boss's priorities. If there is a mismatch, it will probably have a negative impact on your evaluation or promotion. You should schedule a conversation with your boss that goes something like this: "Boss, I am enthusiastic, and I am committed. I am happy to be at this firm. And I am happy to be on your team. When I look back over the last 90 days, my three biggest accomplishments were A, B, and C. For the next 90 days, I am planning to focus on X, Y, and Z." Then you ask the magic question, "Boss, is that how you want me to spend my time?"

You have just thrown a lighting bolt into the boss's office. You've just woken him or her up[!] It is not that you have a bad boss. You have a busy boss. By using my technique, the boss might say, "X and Y are okay. But what about M?" To which you might reply, "I can do M. I didn't know I was supposed to do M."

I recommend this straightforward approach because too often people end up in my office, all upset that they have spent half a year focused on the wrong priorities. It is important to revisit your job parameters with your boss on a quarterly basis to confirm that you are meeting and exceeding the expectations of your current position. This technique allows you to be forward looking and goal-focused with your boss instead of revisiting previous performance evaluations.

I learned the value of a periodic cup of coffee with the boss the hard way. Earlier in my career, I made three big assumptions about my work and my boss: I assumed that I was working on the right priorities, that my hard work and accomplishments would speak for themselves, and that my boss would proactively tell me when I was off course. All three of my assumptions were wrong.

About halfway through the year, my boss called me in his office to say that I was not doing enough to get new clients versus maintaining our existing client relationships. I was not creating the right amount of high-margin business. My boss had no idea how I was spending my time.

After that experience, I sent my boss a one-page progress report every month. Each progress report said what I was doing to respond to his input. Once a quarter, I asked for a 15-minute cup of coffee. By asking the magic question, "Is this how you want me to spend my time?" I was able either to get my boss to endorse what I was doing or to force my boss to tell me where I was going off track while I still had time to correct.

V

NETWORKING: RISKS, BENEFITS, AND TIPS

If you link your career success to one boss on one career path, your career portfolio will have limited assets. It is the equivalent of buying one lottery ticket in hopes of hitting the jackpot.

Networking is a better approach that can broaden the number of people you know, the number of people who know you, and the number of opportunities you are presented during your career.

People who network are more likely to advance by better connecting the dots to a successful career. Networking is the key to developing relationships, differentiating yourself internally, and expanding your career opportunities. Networking builds your social capital. I think of social capital as the value created based on reciprocity, trust, information and cooperation within your social network.[1] Networking was crucial to me as a junior person in professional services, and it is just as critical to me today.

[1] Sander, Thomas. "About Social Capital". Saguaro Seminar: Civic Engagement in America. John F. Kennedy School of Government at Harvard University. Retrieved December 2, 2015.

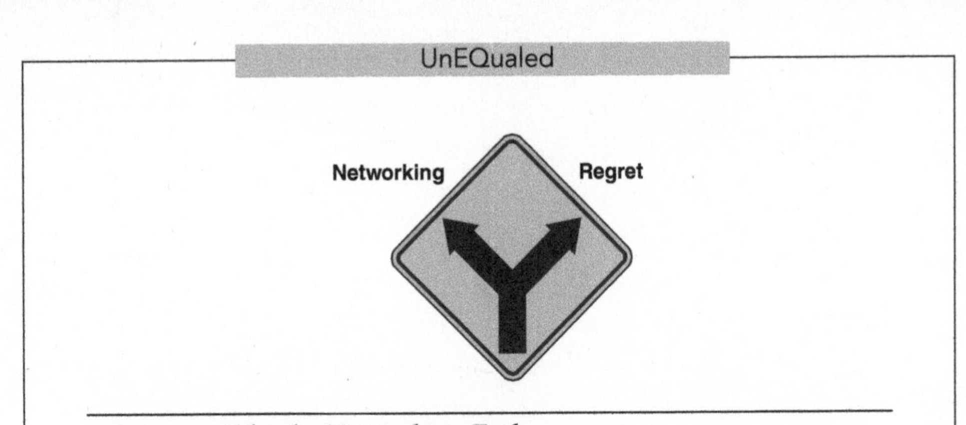

Figure 5.1 Take the Networking Fork

Networking can benefit you at every point in your career and can lead to finding sponsors who can change your career trajectory.

Few people understand how to network effectively and many regret not networking as seen in Figure 5.1. There are many good books about how to network. I like the book *Never Eat Alone* by Keith Ferrazzi and Tahl Raz that provides practical tips about how to leverage the power of relationships and networking to thrive in business.

Even though there are a lot of networking books and people know networking is important, many people avoid networking because they are afraid of rejection. Some people think that if they network, others will find them insincere or overly political or pushy. Other people do not think that they have time for networking or think that they are too junior to begin networking.

The late, great Yankee Yogi Berra said, "When you come to a fork in the road, take it." Every day you come to work, you come to a fork in the road. You can choose to either embrace networking, despite any misgivings or fears about the potential outcomes, or not embrace it. You can choose not to network because you are afraid of the potential outcomes. For example, "I am afraid of being perceived as too political." Or perhaps, "I am afraid of being rejected. I don't want to face the pain of rejection."

However, based on my experience, I am convinced that you will have professional and personal regrets if you do not network.

If you ask people at the end of their lives if they regretted more the risk they took or the risk they did not take, virtually all of them will say they regret the risk they did not take—the girl they didn't ask out, the trip they didn't take, the job they didn't try for. Don't miss the opportunity to network because you are afraid to take the risk.

> "Twenty years from now you will be more disappointed by the things you didn't do than by the ones you did do. So throw off the bowlines. Sail away from the safe harbor. Catch the trade winds in your sails. Explore. Dream. Discover."
>
> *Mark Twain, American author and humorist*

BENEFITS OF NETWORKING

Networking helps you to know more people inside and outside of your firm. That means you will have more people in your network to lean on when you need professional or personal guidance. People with well-developed networks benefit professionally. They find out about new job openings more quickly, do not get trapped in dead-end situations, and find better resources to leverage throughout their career.

Networking is like holding multiple lottery tickets. Networking can help transform you from being a well-kept secret in your firm to being a well-known person with a diversified career portfolio, multiple advocates, a range of opportunities, and many sources of motivation and assistance. Networking is key to identifying new opportunities and advancing your career. Some of the best tips I have received have come from acquaintances in my network rather than those people with whom I was close.

BE SYSTEMATIC

Networking is an ongoing activity; you can always do more to strengthen your network. Be systematic. Keep a list of people in your network, and make sure that you stay in contact with them. I like to connect with everyone in my network at least once every six months. When I am on a plane or commuting to work, I go through my calendar and say, "Okay, this is April. Who did I see last November, so that I know who I am due to catch up with again?"

If I have not worn something in my closet for many months, it is not truly in my wardrobe and those clothes get sent to Goodwill. It is the same thing with networking. If you have not seen someone in six months, you may think they are in your network, but they are not.

Once I figure out the people I need to connect with, I send them a quick email with the subject "Overdue." The email says something like, "Hey, we are overdue. Let's catch up. How about coffee?" And now for the magic words: "No rush." That lets them know that I don't need something from them right now, but I simply want to stay in touch and keep them as part of my network. It is a pretty soft approach, but it is effective.

ICEBREAKERS

If it is your first meeting with someone, particularly if the person is senior to you, you might be concerned that you won't know what to talk about. Just remember that most people's favorite topic is—themselves.

You can ask a question like, "How did you get started in this business?" You are likely to get an eager—and often lengthy—response. Whatever you do, do not interrupt. The more the other person talks, the better you are doing.

This technique works with all kinds of people. If you happened to meet the Pope, you could ask, "How did you get started in religion?" You can use this icebreaker with anybody.

Once you ask the question, be sure to listen carefully to the answer. Eliminate distractions, and make eye contact with the speaker. Nod or use other cues, such as, "Tell me more," to show you're listening—but don't pry. It can be helpful to paraphrase or restate the speaker's points, if needed, to make sure you understand them correctly. Assure the speaker that what he or she is saying will remain confidential.

As you listen, look for common interests and points of connection that you have with this new person. Once you find out what you have in common, you can point out the common interests or connections: "I enjoy Italian movies, too," or, "I like cooking."

Also listen for the person's priorities. If you know what this person is working on, then you can look for articles that might be of interest that you can send to the person. That is a way to begin to build a relationship, and it all begins with the simple question: "How did you get started in this business?"

CURRENCY

It is useful to have "currency" when reaching out to someone in your network. Reciprocity is important for effective networking, so focus on how you can be a resource for others. What benefit will they derive from your relationship? Your ability to help someone in your network depends on the strength of the connections in your network.

If you are working on a project or with a new client, think about what might be topical or interesting to your audience. Then search online through a system such as Google News Alerts to find information on that subject. You can set it up so that you get a daily email from Google with news on that topic. I get up early and read my Google alerts. I frequently find stories that are about to be in that day's newspaper, and I send them to people who would be interested in the story. I get about a 91 percent response rate on sending articles that might be of interest to people in my network.

You also can check finviz.com, which provides aggregated financial research, analysis, and visualization. Under the News tab, the most up-to-date news is in the left-hand column and blogs are down the right-hand side of the page.

I also look for opportunities to send someone a congratulatory email, such as when they have gotten a promotion, won a deal, been mentioned in an article, received an award, and so on. I send a quick email that says, "Hey, way to go. I saw your name in lights." I get a 100 percent response rate on congratulatory emails.

Remember to contact people in your network when they face adversity as well. Often no one reaches out when something bad happens, even when that might be the moment a person most needs the support of a network. People remember who cared about them in bad times.

Finally, take a long-term view of networking. Don't wait until you need something to build your network. Cultivate networking relationships over time, so that they will be there when you need them.

VI

WHERE ARE YOU?

If you are six months into your job, you should pat yourself on the back. Then start to think more about how to objectively evaluate your current position. Consider your boss, your lifestyle, your geographic preferences, and your pay, as shown in Figure 6.1.

You need to be realistic about what you can improve and how you are perceived within your organization and with your clients. Whom you work for should be the most important consideration; your immediate boss will overshadow lifestyle, geographic preferences, and pay. Every position is a mixed bag of likes and dislikes.

Boss: The old adage says that people join great companies and they quit bad bosses. People join great companies for macro reasons like the CEO, the brand, the reputation in the marketplace, the momentum of the company, and so on. Once they join a new company, many people overemphasize their function within that company and underemphasize the importance of a good boss. We will discuss your boss at more length later in the book.

Lifestyle: When evaluating your current spot in terms of lifestyle, is your boss aware of your current lifestyle and the lifestyle you aspire to have?

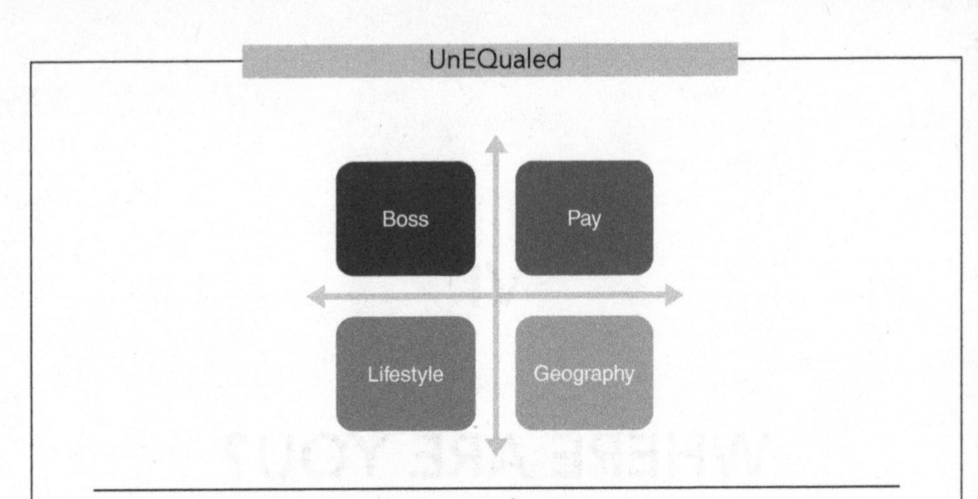

Figure 6.1 Boss, Lifestyle, Geography, Pay

Does your boss have a clue that you are in at 6:30 a.m. or that you are working all-nighters? Does your boss know what work you have on your plate? Your boss may have no idea about the competing priorities that you are juggling.

Does your current boss care about your lifestyle? Is your current boss doing anything to improve your lifestyle? Consider whether your current commitment to your job and your desired lifestyle are compatible. Also, consider how your desired lifestyle may evolve in the future and whether your current post provides you with the flexibility to balance work and life.

Geographic preference: Do you enjoy working in your current location and office, or do you dream of switching to a different geography? What are the career implications of staying in your current location versus switching to a different location? How supportive is your current management of corporate mobility? If you move locations, how easy is it to return to your home office? Time spent in a small regional office could give you a new perspective, new network, and greater responsibility, but be careful because out of sight at the main location can mean out of mind for management at the main location.

Pay: Money matters, but not as much as you may think. The promise of higher pay may motivate you to do better work. However, fair compensation and a strong corporate culture that inspires employees to do their best work and recognizes their contributions may unlock more employee potential and fulfillment than just higher compensation. Employees derive satisfaction from the excitement and challenge of work, believing that they are doing important work and being part of a great team. Most important is feeling valued and respected by the organization. Interestingly, the absence of fair compensation may make you upset, but a pay raise does not necessarily make you happy. Pay can be a message about where you are relative to others. It is important to consider your pay in the context of the other factors that affect your satisfaction with your current assignment.

HOW TO BE HAPPIER

What would make you happier than you are in your current position? I don't advocate job hopping, but I do advocate a periodic and objective review of where you are professionally. What works, and what does not work? What is satisfying, gratifying, and inspiring about your current spot? And what is frustrating? Is there a specific position or a different boss that would make you happier? You need to know where you are in order to navigate where you are going. Only you can answer, "Where am I? And what would make me happier?"

After I had been at Morgan Stanley for about six years, I went to see one of my mentors. I had hit a professional speed-bump, and I wanted his advice. He is a really wonderful, smart guy.

It was a Thursday. I came to my mentor with a variety of complaints that were symptomatic of my need for reassurance and positive reinforcement.

I told my mentor, "I am going to quit." My mentor was surprised but, after he thought about it, he said, "All right, but quit on Monday." I insisted that I was going to quit that day, a Thursday. But my mentor said, "If you wait until Monday and you still want to leave, then I will help you say goodbye and pack your boxes. Between now and Monday, I need you to think about what it is—what gig, what boss, what company, what different job—that would make you happier than you already are. You always want to think about your current position as compared to what else you could do." I agreed to wait.

On Monday I walked into his office and said I had decided to stay. I said, "I couldn't think of what was going make me happier." My mentor said, "Hooray. Get over yourself. This will work out." The word *happier* had really made a big impression on me. He did not say *wealthier*; he said *happier*.

CREATE A ROADMAP TO YOUR DREAM JOB

> "He who is not courageous enough to take risks will accomplish nothing in life."
>
> *Muhammad Ali, professional boxer*

Whether you want to reach for the corner office or improve your performance in your current job, it helps to create a roadmap outlining the steps you need to take to reach your goals. If you have no destination, any road will get you there. But if you know where you want to go, you need a map.

In order to create your career roadmap, you need both awareness and willingness. You need to be aware of where you are today, you need to know your skill gaps and have a realistic understanding of your limitations, and you should be aware of your potential and have knowledge of opportunities that you might like to pursue.

You need a heavy dose of willingness because without the willingness to network, to improve your skill set, and to take career risk, you will not get your dream gig and you might end up marginalized and overlooked for a promotion. Don't rely completely on your immediate boss to promote you. If something happens to your boss, no one will know you or your work.

When you are thinking about your dream job, be as objective as you can about yourself. Be realistic about your aspirations and capabilities. And talk to people whom you really trust to validate that your dream makes sense for you.

For example, I love baseball and the New York Yankees. But if I asked the Yankees' manager for a spot on his roster, he would laugh. I could have all the desire and willingness in the world, but I could not play for the Yankees.

Sometimes you have a choice in your next job between a promotion at your current firm and a position at a competitor. In general, when people move inside their firm, they get a pay increase and usually an increase in responsibility, which can expand their role. When people move to a new firm, they might receive a bigger pay increase, but often they do not get increased responsibilities.

In other words, the choice often is whether you want to move up the ranks with your current employer or you want to perform the same function for more money at another outfit. There can be many valid reasons to leave your current firm, but I believe strongly that money alone is not enough. You need to look at the long-term impact on your career. In my experience, job hoppers are often viewed as self-serving hired guns, while people who move within the same firm demonstrate commitment, develop a strong network, know who the best bosses are, and understand the firm's strategy and culture.

NAVIGATING THE HEADWINDS AND TAILWINDS OF YOUR CAREER

I am a transportation banker at Morgan Stanley, and I was a Navy engineer. As a result, I think in terms of mapping and destinations. Whether you are flying an airplane or trying to get from your current job to that dream job, you can face headwinds or tailwinds. When it comes to your career path, there are three factors that will either help speed you up or retard your ability to get to your destination. Those factors are networking, metrics, and culture.

Networking: If you do not have a strong network or relationships, then no one will tell you when a new opportunity opens up, or you may make the wrong choice if you try to switch positions on your own. For example, you might read an official announcement that your dream job has just gone to another person, and you didn't even know the position was open.

If you had a strong network, then you would have gotten the heads-up that your dream job was about to become available, and you could have put your name into consideration for that job. You want to be aware of any openings at your firm before the email goes out announcing that someone else is getting your dream spot.

Even if you have built a strong network, you can suffer a setback in your career by not recognizing the importance of consulting your network before making a decision. For example, perhaps a senior person calls you and says the firm is transferring Joe to the London office and management thinks you should step up to take Joe's current job. Without thinking about it or talking to your network, you say, "Great, I'm in!" Then 20 minutes after the official announcement of your new position, you find yourself fielding a barrage of phone calls and emails saying some variation of, "You idiot. What were you thinking, taking Joe's seat? Why didn't you talk to me first? Everybody knows that Joe's boss is a disaster." Now you find yourself stuck with no easy way out. If you pause and consult your network before making a big career decision, then you can avoid this kind of a situation. A solid network can provide you with personal, social, and emotional support to identify the right dream job, and then to get it.

Metrics: Do you know the performance evaluation criteria and your manager's expectations for your current role? Most professional services firms have published the performance evaluation criteria by level. That allows you to offer examples of how you have achieved what is asked of you at your level or how you are prepared to achieve at the next level.

Culture: Every organization has a distinct corporate culture. Since many professional services employees spend long hours working, their firm's culture has a significant effect on both their work and personal lives. Corporate culture is a critical factor in the success of your firm. If you want to thrive in your firm, you need to understand your firm's corporate culture and learn to navigate it seamlessly. We discuss values and corporate culture more in Part 3 of this book.

VII

SELLING YOURSELF

When you work in a professional services firm, it is essential to have an elevator pitch—a synopsis of your business or role in a version that is short enough to fit in the time between floors in an elevator. An elevator pitch is extremely important for long-term success.

Imagine that it is 7:30 p.m. and you are in the elevator alone when the doors open and the head of your firm walks into the elevator. Are you going to take this opportunity to introduce yourself and impress the head of your firm, or are you going to demonstrate how well you can avoid eye contact by looking at your smartphone?

This is precisely why you need to have prepared an elevator pitch. It is just 25 words, or three sentences.

Your elevator pitch should:

- Be concise
- Be enthusiastic
- Clearly state your name and role
- Ask a question

Anyone should be able to understand your role after hearing your elevator pitch. Avoid buzzwords or jargon in your elevator pitch; they can confuse the listener and make you sound pompous. Do not say anything confidential in your elevator pitch. If you have time and your listener's attention, ask a question in order to gauge the listener's level of interest in the conversation. Based on the response to your question, you can further tailor your message.

If your elevator pitch is clear, concise, and appealing, it encourages the person you are speaking with to think about ways they might be able to work with you or promote what you do to others. Try practicing your elevator pitch on a friend who knows little about your firm or what you do. If the friend gets it, then you have an effective elevator pitch.

You never know who will step into the elevator when the door opens. In my career, I have been on elevators with Bill Gates, former President Ronald Reagan, Michael Dell, Henry Paulson, and Alan Greenspan. You also don't know who will sit next to you on an airplane or stand beside you while you wait to board a plane; my list includes Willie Mays, Sir Paul McCartney, Pete Sampras, Andre Agassi, Katie Couric, Ron Howard, and Diane Sawyer.

On an airplane, you have more time than you have on an elevator. And since each situation is extemporaneous, you can't have a canned script every time. Never talk about the weather. Ask the other person about himself or herself. If you have something in common, that really helps. Be optimistic, assume rapport, and introduce yourself.

SPEAK UP

Speaking up can improve people's perceptions of you. An old friend once told me, "A viewpoint is worth 20 IQ points." If you go to a meeting and don't speak up, people will leave the meeting assuming you have nothing to say.

An important part of the impression you make in a meeting is your stage or executive presence. On your way to the meeting, take a moment to check how you look in front of a mirror. When you walk into the conference room, ensure you look and act organized and professional. Remember the cliché: You don't get a second chance to make a strong first impression.

By arriving early, you will get a seat at the conference table. Act confidently. Speak loudly enough to be heard. Do not fold your arms. Look others in the eye. Sit straight and lean forward slightly. It gets harder to speak as the meeting progresses, so try to establish your voice early. Whatever you do, don't raise your hand and ask, "Can I say something?" Don't say, "This might not work but maybe . . . ."

If your mentor is attending the meeting, ask your mentor beforehand to call on you to ask your point of view. If your mentor is not attending the meeting, don't wait for someone to turn the floor over to you, as you might be waiting the whole meeting. Inserting yourself into the conversation and speaking with confidence takes courage, but offers big rewards.

Suppose you are in a meeting with a senior person at your firm. You can wait until the senior person is about 92 percent finished and then say, "You know, I agree with Mr. Senior Person. And furthermore . . . ."

Now, Mr. Big Shot has two choices. He can either let you talk or he can tell you that you can talk when he is done. Either way, you get the opportunity to speak. But the most important part of this scenario is to wait until the senior person is almost finished talking.

Then start by saying, "I agree with Mr. Senior Person." People like it when someone agrees with what they are saying. After that, though, don't be afraid to say what you think. The challenge is to have confidence in what you have prepared to share and then to not censor yourself when you get the chance to share it. But you have to figure out how to start.

Begin by saying something like, "Have we thought about X?" "Did anyone mention Y?" "Is it worth revisiting Z?"

Before the client meeting, look for opportunities to practice articulating your thoughts. Internal preparation meetings can provide a good forum to test out your ideas before the big meeting. Not only will you gain confidence in your own ability to present and defend your point of view, but you will also gain the confidence and trust of your colleagues while making the whole team more prepared for the meeting.

VIII

THE PATH TO SPONSORSHIP

Chapter 5 introduced the importance of networking. I think of networking as creating a foundation of relationships from which you can identify role models. As you add role models to your network, mentors will emerge who can provide advice and coaching and spot new opportunities for you. From those mentors, you will find sponsors who invest their personal capital in you and take action to open new doors for you to advance your career. This is depicted in the Sponsorship Pyramid in Figure 8.1.

ROLE MODELS

A subset of your network will be your role models. From networking, you can start to home in on who might be a good role model for you. A role model is someone you identify with, someone who inspires you and someone you aspire to be like: "If she can do it, I can do it. If I can present like her or persuade clients like her, then I can succeed like her." If your role model is a senior person at your firm, you need to take the initiative to have that senior person be part of your network so that you can get to know that person better.

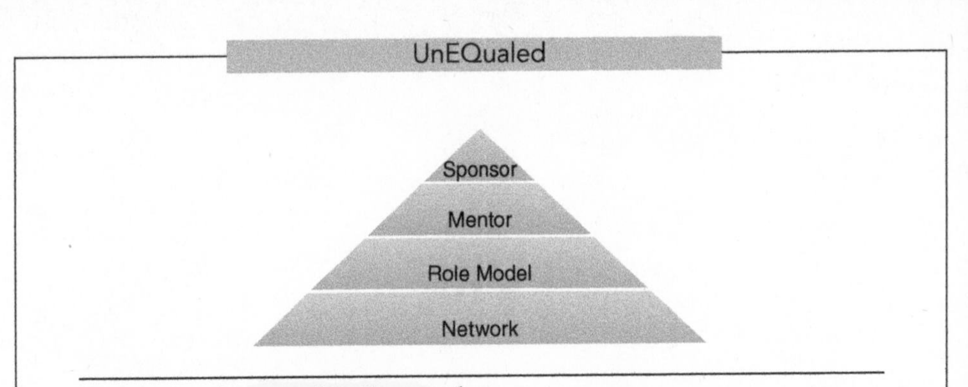

Figure 8.1 Sponsorship Pyramid

When I was starting out, we had an informal apprentice model where we learned investment banking by paying very close attention to how more experienced people behaved in front of clients. By watching my role models, I learned how to balance decisions between choosing what was right for the client and the firm in the long term and what was helpful for my career in the short term.

A role model can help you with the following:

- *Provide valuable advice.* Role models can be your guide and sounding board for ideas. They can help you decide on the best course of action in difficult situations.
- *Develop knowledge and skills.* Role models can help you identify the skills and expertise you need to succeed. They may teach you what you need to know or advise you on where to go for the information you need.
- *Improve communication skills.* My role models taught me how to write, speak, and act with clients.
- *Enhance appearance.* Since most of my early work experience was in the military, my role models showed me how to present myself and carry myself professionally.

MENTORS

As you strengthen your relationships with your role models, mentors will emerge. While role models are essentially passive—you learn from them by observing what they do—mentors take an active interest in your development. A mentor is someone who is willing to use his or her experience to guide you through the organization and to provide advice and guidance for your career. In *The Odyssey*, Odysseus entrusted the care of his son, Telemachus, to Mentor when Odysseus set out to fight the Trojan War.

Mentors are helpful as you start to define your career aspirations. They can help you determine and articulate your strengths: what you do well and what differentiates you from others at your level. The best mentors will help you learn from their mistakes and thus help you avoid making those same mistakes on your own. Mentors can tell you how others in your organization perceive you. They can see opportunities for you that you cannot see for yourself. A well-chosen mentor also can help you navigate the firm's unwritten rules.

In identifying potential mentors, I approached people I respected and told them that I admired their judgment and would like to learn from them. Some of the topics that I would discuss with my potential mentors included business etiquette, dressing for success, networking, presentation skills, and delivering a difficult message to a client.

I have been fortunate to have had several mentors in my life and career. All of my mentors shared several characteristics:

- They were willing to share their wisdom and expertise.
- They were optimistic and empathetic.
- They helped me through tough times and showed me how to find perspective.
- The best mentors I had did one or more of the following:
    - Motivated me to accomplish more than I thought I could.
    - Believed in me and did not let me give up on myself.
    - Told me the truth, even when it hurt—but always did so in private.

I have had many mentors throughout my life. In my professional career, they were basically teachers with relevant investment banking experience.

But there also were important mentors who helped me to develop personal values and showed me how to be the kind of adult I wanted to be. My early mentors included my mom and dad, who instilled in me the value of faith, education, and teamwork; my high school football coach, Mike Farley, who taught me the desire to win is useless without the desire to prepare; and Father Paul Prucha S.J., who encouraged me to serve others.

SPONSORS

Mentors are good, but sponsors are even better. Mentors give you advice when it is just the two of you. Sponsors talk positively about you to others and take action in advancing your career.

A sponsor could be your boss or someone you work with closely. It is a big task to find someone who is willing to be your sponsor. Sponsors put their name out there for you, put their personal brand on you, invest in you, and stick their neck out for you. Your sponsor makes a significant investment in advancing your career. A sponsor connects you to important people and assignments that can open new doors for you and help guide you through your career.

One of the several times I did not get promoted to managing director, I happened to have lunch with a prominent lawyer. I was complaining about how upsetting it was that I did not get promoted. The lawyer said, "So Runde, when they made the promotion decision yesterday, there was a promotion committee that met, right?" I said, "Yeah." He said, "Well, were you in the room?" I said, "Of course I was not in the room. They were talking about me." He said, "Okay. What is going to happen a year from yesterday? The same group is going to meet and talk about you?"

"Yeah," I said. He said, "Are you going be in the room next year this time?" I said, "No, you don't get to go to a meeting when they talk about you." He said, "Okay. So who is going to talk about you a year from now? And what are they going to say about you?" "Oh," I said, "I have no idea."

The lawyer said, "You have a lot of work to do. You have to find a sponsor or sponsors. You have to work your tail off for the next 365 days to find your sponsor and give that person the ammunition to truthfully say what needs to be said about your promotion, because you are not going to be in the room next year, either. If you do not find a sponsor and help the sponsor with the talking points, then the same darn thing is going to happen next year." That was sound advice!

IX

MAGIC FORMULA

"For of all sad words of tongue or pen,
The saddest are these: "It might have been!"

John Greenleaf Whittier, poet, "Maud Miller"

There is a magic formula for success in professional services: ability, opportunity, and courage.

ABILITY

In today's fast-paced and turbulent world of professional services, it is no longer enough to work long hours and demonstrate proficiency in your respective field. To get ahead as an investment banker, lawyer, consultant, or accountant in today's competitive world, you must find a way to succeed on teams and on projects while also distinguishing yourself as an individual. EQ can help you to understand the corporate culture and its unwritten rules, relate to bosses, colleagues, and clients, and become a top-level performer—even in the first year on the job.

OPPORTUNITY

Employment opportunities come to you through your immediate boss and your network. If you master the parameters of your current job, then your boss should identify opportunities that will allow you to grow your skill set and motivate you to progress. A good boss will help you to map a career growth plan and provide opportunities for you to step up. These new opportunities will allow you to expand your skill set, confidence, and competencies. This could mean increased exposure to clients, more responsibility on an engagement, an opportunity to lead a team, and so on.

If you have a solid network, then you will find out when a new opportunity is about to arise and you can check a new job offer with people in your network to make sure that you are making a wise decision.

COURAGE

> "Courage is what it takes to stand up and speak; courage is also what it takes to sit down and listen."
>
> *Winston Churchill, United Kingdom prime minister*

Mentors and sponsors can give you courage to succeed in your career. Mentors are willing to use their experience to help you navigate through your organization and to provide advice and guidance for your career. They can help you determine and articulate your strengths—what you do well and what differentiates you from others at your level. Mentors can tell you how others in your organization perceive you. They can see opportunities for you that you cannot see for yourself. Unlike a mentor, a sponsor will take a risk on you, has the power or authority to put you in a higher position, and is there for you when you need someone to back you up. A sponsor will connect you to important players and assignments that will open new doors for you and help guide you through your career.

Even the best mentors cannot assist you if you do not have the courage to tell them your concerns and fears. Telling anyone you feel confused or inadequate requires enough humility to show your vulnerability. The right mentor can help you discover your inner strength and provide you the extra dose of confidence you need to make the right decision, move forward, or face reality rather than live in denial. Do you remember the lion in *The Wizard of Oz*, who went to see the great and powerful wizard? The lion thought he lacked courage, but his real problem was that he did not believe in himself. The wizard, acting as a mentor, gave the lion a medal marked "courage," which was just the confidence boost the lion needed. Acknowledge your concerns and fears when talking with your mentor. Be open to discussing those issues with your mentor and listen to the advice your mentor gives you.

2

BECOMING MORE COMMERCIAL (HOW TO WORK WITH YOUR CLIENTS)

X

WHY IS BEING COMMERCIAL RELEVANT TO YOU?

Have you ever wondered why being commercial is relevant to you? There was a recent survey conducted by the Association of Graduate Recruiters in the United Kingdom about the most important skills for college graduates entering the workforce in the twenty-first century. I expected that the top skills for graduates would be teamwork and problem solving. I was surprised when I read the survey results. What was the number-one skill that the Association of Graduate Recruiters thought graduates were missing?

The top skill shortage, according to employers across multiple industries, was commercial awareness. Some 67 percent of employers chose commercial awareness over communication, leadership, teamwork, and problem solving (see Table 10.1).

What exactly is commercial awareness? Different employers have different interpretations of what commercial awareness means for their business and industry. Some professional services firms refer to it as the business case for your promotion or your ability to win new business for the firm.

Table 10.1 Top Skill Shortages Among Graduates

Skill	Percent of Employers Surveyed
1. Commercial Awareness	67%
2. Communication	64%
3. Leadership	33%
4. Teamwork	33%
5. Problem Solving	32%

Source: Association of Graduate Recruiters, "Skills for Graduates in the 21st Century".

In general, commercial awareness is an understanding of a business, product, or service; how to create that product or service; and how to ask for and win new business. It is also an understanding of the industry in which the business operates, the major competitors, and how those competitors compare and contrast. Commercial awareness helps you succeed in professional services by converting client relationships into revenue.

TURN CLIENT RELATIONSHIPS INTO REVENUE

> "It is necessary for us to learn from others' mistakes. You will not live long enough to make them all yourself."
>
> *Hyman G. Rickover, Admiral, U.S. Navy*

All professional services firms talk about being respected by clients and the importance of building long-term client relationships. A leader at Morgan Stanley once said to a group of investment bankers, "I have been all around the globe, and I have met your clients. And your clients really respect you. You have great client relationships." And then he paused and said, "Now, I need you to turn relationships into revenue."

This was a profound idea, expressed very clearly. I knew that a key part of my job was to build great relationships and to be a trusted adviser. Intuitively, I knew there was also an important commercial aspect to my job.

That day, the speaker vividly reminded me that long-term client relationships are simply assets, and those assets are only worth something if they are turned into revenue. Professional services firms are in business to do business; they are not in business just to build relationships. I had never quite understood that before that conversation.

This was a hard lesson to learn. I do not want you to make the same mistake in thinking that your job is only to build relationships. Your job is also to turn client relationships into revenue.

HOW TO BE MORE COMMERCIAL

There is an art to navigating client relationships and converting those relationships into revenue. There are many people in professional services firms who are not able to monetize their client relationships. There are many others who do not understand the delicate balance of managing long-term client relationships, personal and professional integrity, and serving the best interests of their clients.

Some people have great client relationships, build strong professional networks, and belong to all the right organizations. Having all these assets does not always mean that you can generate revenue. For example, I worked with a guy named Dan who was a great golfer, a really nice guy, and a member at all of the right clubs. Everyone loved Dan. He was great at creating long-term client relationships. However, Dan could not ask for business or convert the client relationship into revenue for the firm. As a result, Dan eventually was eased out of the firm and replaced by another banker who could turn relationships into revenue.

Other people are great at executing the technical aspects of professional services firm work. However, these people rarely create new revenue opportunities for their firms because they are waiting for the client to call them or they are waiting for a colleague to produce the next transaction so they can execute it. In a professional services firm, being reactive to a client request is not as valuable as proactively recognizing a valuable strategic opportunity for a client and thus generating new revenue for the firm.

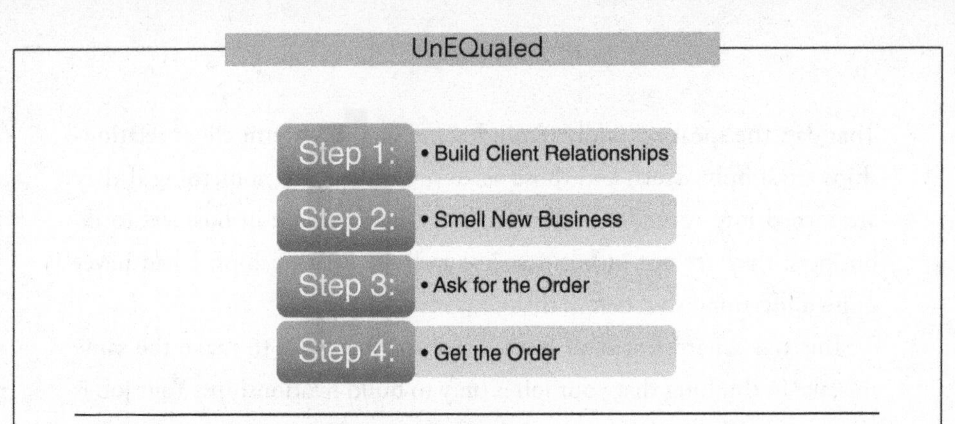

Figure 10.1 Steps to Getting the Order

These execution-oriented professionals need to be more aggressively looking for new business and get more closely in touch with their clients.

A commercially successful professional services person needs to build solid client relationships, be able to identify new business, ask for the order, and be awarded the transaction, as shown in Figure 10.1.

There are many people in professional services who can do some of these steps well, but not all of these steps. There are people who have solid client relationships and can anticipate business, but can't ask for the order. There are people who have solid client relationships, can anticipate business and can ask for the order, but they are always the runner-up and never win the business. These people always seem to have an excuse or alibi why they did not win the business. I want to help you so that you can monetize your client relationships and generate revenue for your firm.

To be a long-term success in the client services business, you must be able to subtly turn client relationships into revenue while preserving your integrity and serving the client well. One of the hardest things to do in client services is to turn down business that the client asks you to execute. The litmus test of optimizing between a high-integrity client relationship and being commercial occurs when the client hires you to do something that you are convinced is not in the client's best interest.

For example, say you have a client that wants to acquire a company that makes typewriters. You have to tell your client that buying a typewriter company does not make strategic sense. It is a delicate balance to tell clients that they should not do a transaction because it is not in their long-term interest even though your firm might give up a fee.

Being commercial also has considerable value to you as you progress in your career. In Part 1 of this book, we talked about knowing your firm's performance evaluation criteria. I guarantee you that an important part of the criteria for moving up the promotion ladder is going to be whether you are commercial.

Building solid client relationships and being commercial sometimes requires judgment and nerves of steel.

I did a number of transactions with a well-known businessman I will call Fred. He was a serious collector of American art. Fred was also known as a skillful and successful dealmaker and was highly regarded as a person who often did favors for others, but rarely asked for favors in return.

I was very surprised when Fred called me one day and said, "Jim, I need a favor." I said, "Sure, what can I do for you?" He asked if I had ever been to Sotheby's or Christie's, the top auction houses in New York City. I said no. Fred said, "I figured as much. That is why I called you."

There was an auction the following week at Sotheby's, and he wanted to buy a piece of art that was labeled in the auction catalog as item 18. However, Fred did not want to attend the auction in person because others in the audience would recognize him and that would change the way they would bid against him. "No one will recognize you," he said. Having me bid in his stead would be very helpful. He told me that when I arrived at Sotheby's I should go to the reception desk and show my driver's license, and I would be given a paddle registered to his account. He authorized me to bid up to $2.5 million on item 18. Though being a proxy bidder for a client at an art auction was clearly not in my job description, I agreed to do it. As part of the adventure, I decided to take my wife and teenage daughter with me. They were sworn to secrecy on the art in question and the bidding limit.

When we arrived that afternoon, everything went as planned. The auction was already underway when a Sotheby's employee quietly came to me and discretely handed me a house phone. It was Fred on the line from his hotel in Paris. He had just learned that others would be bidding against me. Fred told me that my limit was now $3 million, but, "if the bidding gets crazy, just use your judgment." He promptly hung up.

I could give no indication of this directive to my wife and daughter. I nervously waited for item 18 to go on the block. The auctioneer started the bidding on item 18 at $2 million. I bid $2.1 million, and there was a bid away from me at $2.2 million. Then, the biddings seesawed back and forth. Quickly the bid was $2.4 million away and I bid $2.5 million. The other person bid $2.6 million and I promptly bid $2.7 million. Since I had apparently exceeded my limit, my wife and daughter were horrified! The bidding quickly jumped to $3.2 million away from me. My heart was racing. Since Fred had said I should use my judgment, I interpreted that instruction to give me a 10 percent cushion and therefore I counterbid at $3.3 million. My family was staring at me as if I had gone mad. We won the bidding for item 18 at $3.3 million. At this point, people were staring at me and wondering who I was. I was an unknown, just as Fred had expected.

After quickly explaining myself to my family, I went to the Sotheby's lobby and called Fred's assistant, Mary Ann. I told her since it was 10 p.m. in Paris, I did not want to disturb Fred. I asked her to please tell Fred that we won item 18 and paid $3.3 million. Mary Ann said, "You were only supposed to spend $2.5 million. You should tell him yourself," and she instantly forwarded the call to Fred. He picked up immediately, and when I told him what had happened, the phone line went quiet.

After what seemed like an eternity, Fred finally said, "Runde, you did the right thing. Thank you."

You never know what it will take to move your client relationships to the next level. Be prepared for surprises, trust your judgment, and above all, keep an open mind.

XI

HOW TO WIN BUSINESS

> "Ego can make you assume that your competition is not as good as it actually is, and that is a recipe for disaster."
>
> *Paul B. Brown, author*

An important way to show that you are commercial is to win a contest for new business. Sometimes a client decides to create a formal process to award a specific transaction. This contest can be called a *pitch*, a *bake-off*, or a *beauty contest*. The process is sometimes initiated by a document called a *request for proposals* (RFP). An RFP is a solicitation, often made through a bidding process, by a company interested in the procurement of service, to potential service providers to submit business proposals.

A *bake-off* is a situation in which several firms compete for a client's business. If you want to be successful commercially, you must realize winning bake-offs is an art and a science. There is a lot at stake. If you are the incumbent adviser, winning will solidify your relationship with the client as you work together to solve an important problem. Winning also can broaden the number of connections between client employees and your colleagues while helping your firm earn important revenues and expand its reputation. On a personal basis, being on the winning team will expand your skill set and enhance your commercial reputation. Some incumbents will make the mistake of having a chip on their shoulder because they resent being asked to compete for a deal they believe they have a right to receive rather than go through a competitive process. On the other hand, if you are a second-tier adviser, the *pitch* is a chance to leapfrog the competition, especially the incumbent adviser. Think of your approach to pitches as part opportunity, part threat.

Having been part of over 100 beauty contests, I have learned that your focus must be on what the client is buying rather than on what you are selling. It is crucial to engage the client emotionally as well as rationally. The emphasis should be on preparation, effective communication, and persuasion. A pitch is not won on hand gestures, posture, or PowerPoint slides. Let the real you shine through because they are hiring you, your team, and your ideas, not a firm or an office building or even your credentials. This process is more about the *who* than the *why*.

Several thematic guidelines will help you deliver the *who* and not just the *why* to the client. In its most basic form, selling is about the product, its benefits, overcoming the client's objections, and creating a call to action. In a pitch, I suggest the time allotment shown in Table 11.1.

Too many pitches are 80 percent credentials and hard-to-read graphics and tables. The tone of a winning pitch is "can do" and user friendly. You should act as an adviser or partner, not a vendor. Talk about the positive outcome the client wants rather than all the technicalities that could interfere or the "plumbing" that will be required. Subtly shape the selection

Table 11.1 Pitch Time Allocations

Topic	% of Time
Product (your team and credentials)	20%
Benefits to the client	40%
How you will work together	15%
Overcoming objections/questions	20%
Call to action	5%

criteria to fit your strategies. This means addressing their questions in a manner that uses your strengths as the solution. Use language such as, "If I were in your shoes, I would think about . . . ." You can also describe how another client facing a similar issue found your expertise in a certain dimension to be highly valuable. Value is so important because it, along with the emotional connection, is a critical differentiator. If you fail to differentiate, then you and your firm become a commodity—and that means the sale becomes about price, not value.

It is critical to demonstrate your value and focus tactically as well. You will create a positive impression if you are professional and organized. Being late for a bake-off is a black mark of arrogance and looks sloppy. Arrive early and get settled. The presentation should be well rehearsed, so it is crisp. Finish early enough to take questions and address any client objections. Typical objections would be, "Your competition says you have a conflict of interest," or "You are too expensive," or "We are too small to get priority focus from your firm."

Your team should have a checklist or step-by-step timeline covering two weeks before the pitch, one week before, the day before, the day of, and the day after. This creates accountability for who does what and when.

In the presentation, speak in the voice of the client. Try to use their lingo rather than jargon (the client will be reluctant to say they do not understand your words). Good sources of "client-speak" are the RFP document and the client's website. This requires advance homework but it is worth doing because it can create a subliminal connection with the client as they will sense rapport.

Consider a one-page executive summary at the beginning of the presentation. It gives the client a roadmap of what will be covered as well as the key takeaways. The summary can be a catalyst at the beginning of the presentation for the client to coach you if the issue has changed or to tell you if they want you to address a subject not mentioned in your summary or in their RFP.

A common mistake is to delegate the presentation to junior staff and to tell them to simply update your standard pitch-book and put the client's logo on the cover. In this scenario, the senior person's first look at the material could be on the plane en-route to the client meeting. This approach almost certainly means the pitch is not custom tailored to the client. Clients can smell a generic presentation.

Another mistake is to underestimate the competition. Some competitors are "economical with the truth." They will exaggerate their own capabilities, promise outlandish valuation outcomes, or fabricate conflicts of interest that restrict your involvement in this process. Other competitors will offer cut-rate pricing. Being the last presentation at a bake-off is a very important defense against these schemes because it gives you a chance to set the record straight.

Making a personal connection was the key to the most important transaction I ever did. It involved the biggest corporate IPO in history at that time. I was part of a 20-person team that had spent about five years creating a solid relationship at all levels of the client except the CEO. We were told the CEO did not deal with bankers and was very skeptical about taking the company public. After all that time and effort, the IPO solution suddenly gained momentum. We were told that the deal was ours to lose and there would not be a beauty contest if we could convince the CEO that an IPO was beneficial to the company and would not harm its culture. Six different officers had cautioned me that at this crucial meeting it would be a disaster if we were too pushy or created a false sense of urgency.

The scene was a hotel conference room several miles from the company headquarters. On one side of the table were the CEO and three of his lieutenants. On our side of the table were a senior colleague from the capital markets group and myself. The tension in the room was palpable and the CEO sat with his arms crossed, which is unfavorable body language. Everyone knew that I had to address the "pushy" issue but I told no one what I was going to say.

I told them that this meeting reminded me of a conversation I had over the weekend. On Sunday, I called my uncle to say hello because he was dying of cancer. In her teenage years our daughter was an accomplished harp player. She happened to be practicing in the background as I made the phone call. (At this point in my story the lieutenants and my colleagues were looking at me as if I had lost my mind.)

My uncle answered the phone, and we chatted. At some point, I said, "Can you hear the music?" He said "What?" I said, "Can you hear the harp?" He said, "Don't rush me." The conference room went silent.

Everyone looked at the CEO. He paused and gave a big laugh. He got it! He knew that we understood not to be pushy or try to rush him into a decision. We won the business.

Perception is everything in a business selection process. The winner is decided by how beautiful the client thinks you are rather than how beautiful you think you are.

THE ART OF BUILDING CLIENT RELATIONSHIPS

As discussed earlier, a professional adviser must walk the tightrope of giving high-integrity advice while being commercial. There is an art to building trust-based, loyal client relationships (see Figure 11.1). It takes many years of apprenticing with experienced client services professionals to really understand how to develop and maintain long-term client relationships. This section of the book will give you the tips that I learned through 40 years of serving clients.

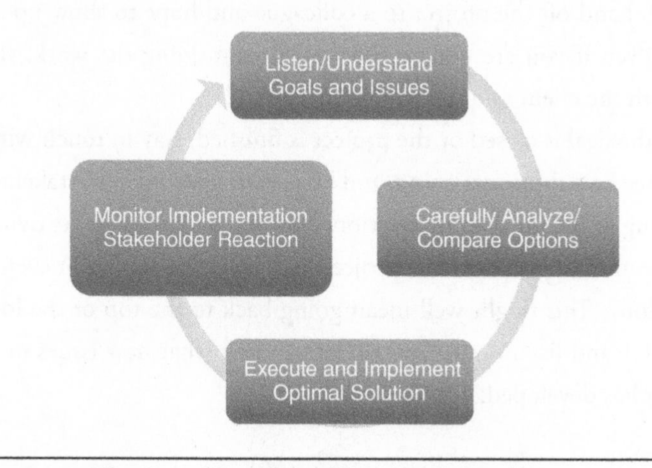

Figure 11.1 The Art of Building Client Relationships

When building client relationships, it is important to listen to and understand your client's goals and issues. Clients have to trust you before they will tell you their goals and issues. They have to perceive that you have their best interests at heart. Empathy allows you to build trust with your clients. Empathy is understanding what others are feeling because you have experienced it yourself or can put yourself in their shoes.

Once you understand their goals and issues, then you can carefully analyze a range of options for the client and compare and contrast those options. It is important that you not jump to the answer with the client. You want to be able to walk the client through a range of alternatives that your team has analyzed and get the client's input on the alternatives.

You want to be an adviser who really understands your client's needs and is working in the client's best interests. If you come in pushing a particular solution, you could be perceived as a self-serving product pusher rather than a trusted adviser who really understands your client's needs. You are not a used car salesperson simply pushing to close this deal. You want a loyal client who will come back again and again with their problems.

When your client has selected the optimal solution to address the goals and issues, then it is your job to execute and implement that solution in a first-class way. High-quality execution requires care and expertise. Be careful not to hand off the project to a colleague and hope to show up at the closing. Even if you are not on the actual team doing the work, stay in touch with the client and the working group.

After the deal is closed or the project is finished, stay in touch with the client to see how things are going, and be alert to how different stakeholders are reacting to the finished transaction. Business and markets are dynamic, which means that over time the project may need fine tuning or even need to be redone. This might well mean going back to the top of the loop of Figure 11.1 and listening to and understanding what new issues or goals the client has developed.

HOW TO MONETIZE CLIENT RELATIONSHIPS

Most professional services firms have a client relationship model rather than a transactional model. The client relationship model is based on the ability to form long-term client relationships that create repeat business. There is strategic and economic importance to repeat business for a professional services firm.

Creating a long-term client relationship requires a significant investment in time and cost at the front end of the client relationship. The relationship model is attractive to professional services firms because the marginal cost of each piece of repeat business becomes smaller and smaller over time.

There are other important benefits to repeat business. Repeat clients often use a variety of your firm's services, thereby introducing many of their people to your people. Also, they can give insight to various strategic and financial issues within the client. Repeat customers are an excellent source of referrals and testimonials. They sometimes will give you unvarnished feedback about how you and your firm can improve your service. Finally, they can give you tips about what your competition is doing or not doing.

Figure 11.2 shows how a client-centered relationship model works.

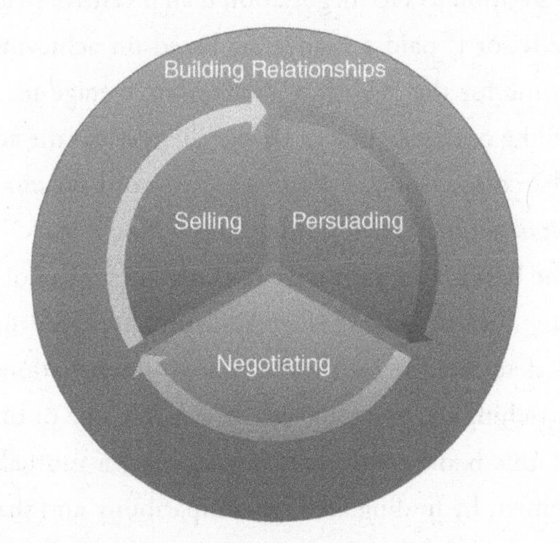

Figure 11.2 Client Relationship Diagram

The overarching goal of such a model is to be continually building and strengthening your relationships with clients. Within this larger goal, when you are interacting with clients you are doing one of three things: persuading, negotiating, or selling. You need to be self-aware enough to know where you are working in the client relationship diagram. I have learned the hard way that those three things each have to be done in a way that preserves the long-term client relationship.

You must learn and understand the fine art of how to persuade, negotiate, and sell.

- *Persuading:* Persuading is subjective. Persuading is more about making an emotional connection with a client. We will talk more about persuading in the next section.
- *Negotiating:* Negotiating is objective; it is about hammering out the terms of the deal with the client. In negotiations, both parties are willing to give some things up in order to get the things they want most. I have learned that one should approach a negotiation as a discussion of a problem or issue in search of a solution rather than as a fixed pie to be divided. A simple example of a creative solution to a fee negotiation is an incentive structure whereby the advisor is paid a higher fee based on achieving an excellent outcome for the client rather than an average fee for creating a middling outcome. The more the client trusts the advisor, the easier the conversation. I try to use the word *discussion* rather than *negotiation* when having these talks with clients.

  The best book that I have read on the subject of negotiating is *Getting to Yes* by Roger Fisher, William Ury, and Bruce Patton. The book describes the nature and tactics of negotiations. Rather than approaching negotiations as a zero-sum game or one winner/one loser, this book emphasizes how to find a mutually satisfactory agreement by finding areas of compatibility and shared interests.
- *Selling:* I think of selling as more about convincing the client that the benefits of an idea, product, or service are worth the cost.

> Persuading and selling are different, but it is a subtle difference. Persuading is more emotional—getting clients to believe that they need a particular solution. Selling is about getting them to pull the trigger on the deal you have reached during the negotiation phase.

Once again, I want you to learn from my mistakes. Sometimes I have not been able to see the forest for the trees in a challenging client situation. You need to be self-aware enough to know when you are negotiating and when you are selling. You can get too close to the line and push too hard. There have been times I pushed too hard on a fee negotiation with a client. Do you know what happened? I blew up the client relationship because I thought it was really important to get the last dollar in the fee negotiation. This is one way I learned the importance of the outer circle versus the inner circle in Figure 11.2: You need to persuade, negotiate, and sell while at the same time building and maintaining the long-term client relationship.

After something went wrong with a client, I would have a conversation with my boss, who would say something like: "You idiot, what were you doing? You were pushing too hard in negotiating the fee, and in the process you blew up a client relationship that has taken decades to develop. What were you thinking?" Not a good idea.

More than once, I decided to work through a tricky client situation on my own, without bringing anyone else from the firm into the boat with me. This was an even worse idea.

If you find yourself getting into some hot water in a client conversation, call a colleague and ask, "Hey, this client situation is about to get difficult. If you were in my shoes, how would you handle this?" Or, "Have you ever seen a situation like this?" Or, "Do you know anybody there?" Or, "How important is this fee versus maintaining the client relationship?" More often than not, someone not as close to the situation can provide useful perspective and different ideas on how to break the impasse. You do not want to be the lone wolf who blows up the client relationship, so that everybody comes back later saying, "If this relationship was in danger, why didn't you reach out for help?"

Any time that you are working with a client, you need to know where you are on the Client Relationship Diagram. Are you persuading, negotiating, or selling? Are you selling in such an aggressive way that you are going to destroy the entire client relationship? Do you need to call in your colleagues so that you can get different perspectives and so you are not perceived as the lone wolf? This is really important, because you always need to think about the outer circle and maintaining the long-term client relationship.

HOW TO BETTER PERSUADE OTHERS

> "It is wise to persuade people to do things and make them think it was their own idea."
>
> *Nelson Mandela, South African politician and philanthropist*

Persuading or influencing others is challenging. Persuasion is different from both negotiation and selling. Persuasion is about making an emotional connection to a client. It is subjective.

Robert Cialdini, considered a leading social scientist in the field of influence, created the Six Principles of Influence:[1]

1. *Reciprocation:* People tend to return a favor. For example: "I did a trade or analysis for you; now would do this for me?"
2. *Commitment and consistency:* People have a deep desire to be consistent. Once you have committed to something, then you are more inclined to go through with it. For example, a client would be more likely to support a new proposal if that client had shown initial interest in the proposal in a large meeting.
3. *Social proof:* People will do things that they see other people are doing. This principle relies on the sense of "safety in numbers"

[1]Robert B. Cialdini, *Influence: Science and Practice* (5th ed.) (New York: Allyn and Bacon, 2008).

or "getting on the bandwagon." For example: "You should really do this trade because everyone is doing it."

4. *Liking:* People like to do business with people they like and are more likely to be influenced by people they like. Clients have to perceive that you have their best interests at heart and that you are not giving self-serving advice: "You like me. I like you. We trust each other. Trust me. This is a good thing for you."
5. *Authority:* People feel a sense of duty or obligation to those in positions of authority. For example: "I'm an expert. I just wrote an article about this. I just gave a speech about this." People are more likely to agree with a credentialed person.
6. *Scarcity:* Perceived scarcity generates demand. One of my favorite examples: "The regulators are about to close this structure down. You better hurry up, because you are going to miss it." Or: "The convertible bond window is about to close; you'd better hurry."

You can use Cialdini's principles whenever you want to persuade or influence others.

Irrespective of how persuasive or insightful you are, your clients will appreciate gratitude. In other words, after you persuade clients to work with you, be sure to thank them. Send a hand written thank-you note after a big assignment is completed. Be authentic. A client who feels sincerely appreciated is likely to be a loyal client. Tell your client, "We value our relationship with you."

XII

HOW TO PREPARE FOR THE CLIENT MEETING

> "Success depends upon previous preparation, and without such preparation there is sure to be failure."
>
> *Confucius*

When you are preparing for a client meeting, think about the 4 *Rs*: *read, reach, raise,* and *ready,* as shown in Figure 12.1.

THE FOUR *Rs*

Read everything that you can find on the company, the sector, and the people you are meeting with as well as the particular issue you might be asked to address. Understand the fundamentals of the client's sector. Does size matter? How is this company positioned? Think about an interesting and different angle to the client meeting.

Reach out to anyone who could provide insights about or contacts at the client. Develop a systematic process for initiating client coverage, including doing reconnaissance. Leverage the network within your firm, including

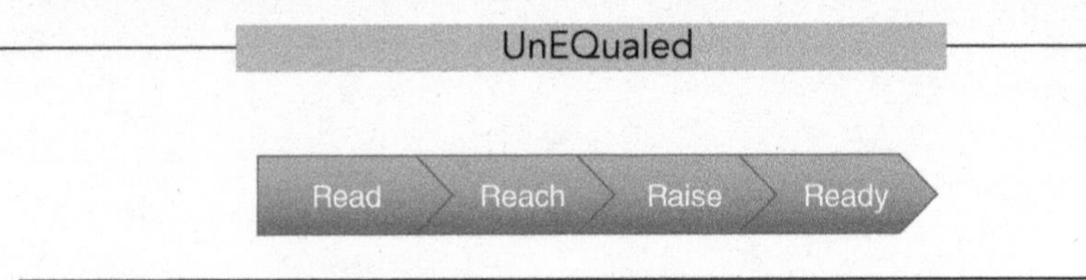

Figure 12.1 How to Prepare for the Client Meeting

senior people who can make relationship connections or provide insights about the client. Identify the key decision makers at the client, other external advisers to the client (e.g., lawyers, accountants, financial advisers, consultants), and important board relationships.

Raise your sights. This means taking some risk and trying to get the first meeting with the chief executive officer or the chief financial officer. In other professional services, it could be the general counsel or the head of strategy. Try for the most senior person possible, because this first meeting sets your level of interaction at your new client.

Too many times, I took the easy path and made the meeting with the Treasurer. What's wrong with that? The Treasurer is a gatekeeper who might say, "You don't need to meet with my boss. Just give me your ideas. I'll make sure you get the credit." Then you are stuck in the Treasurer's office. It is hard to move up if you go in too low with your first meeting. It is risky and scary to start high and move down, but you're much better off starting at a higher vantage point if you can get away with it.

Another gatekeeper can be the assistant. If you call the assistant for a meeting and the assistant asks what the meeting is about, say, "Please tell the boss that I have some *insights* that are going to help him or her do the job better."

The assistant may ask, "Well, what are those insights?" You politely respond, "These insights are too sensitive. I have to tell the boss in person." That is irresistible bait. If you tell the assistant that you have insights that are going to help the boss do a better job, you will get a meeting. Now, you'd better come up with some great insights, because I can virtually guarantee you that you will get a meeting.

Finally, show that you are *ready* and arrive early. First, being early shows respect, in the same way that being late is disrespectful. Plus, if you are early, you can chat up the assistant. You never know what the assistant may tell you. Get to know the assistant. If you are authentically nice to the assistant and have a strong relationship with the assistant, you will be amazed at how helpful an assistant can be to you.

Also, if you are early, you can catch up with other contacts at the client and gather last-minute intelligence before the client meeting.

If the assistant puts you in a conference room before the meeting, you can get centered and organized. When you get into the conference room, it gives you the opportunity to think strategically about the seating dynamics. Seating arrangements in a business meeting are not random and require planning. You do not want to overwhelm the client, and you want to set up a collegial dynamic in the client meeting.

At a rectangular conference table, the power position is in the center of the table facing the door. The person seated there can see who is entering and exiting the room. The people with the most power may jockey for that spot. The second most important position is the seat to the power position's right and the third seat to the power position's left. These seats are known as the *cooperative spots.*

The next most powerful position is at the corner of the table. It allows people who do not know each other to sit close but still have the table's corner as a boundary.

The most competitive seat in relation to the power seat is directly across. The table serves as a natural barrier, and people in meetings who sit across from one another may become almost adversarial during the meeting.

If you are trying to build a relationship with a client, sitting in the corner spot is most advantageous. You do not want to unconsciously create a competitive situation by sitting across from the client.

The worst outcome is if you put yourself at the center of the table facing the door or at the head of the table to show that you are the boss. If you take either of these seats, it is a power play against the client.

The second worst outcome is if the seating creates a "we/they" dynamic. If there are four members of our firm and only one person from the client, then I sit with the client and ask the rest of our team to sit across the table. This seating arrangement implicitly says that I am siding with the client.

The subtle messages you send when you choose where you sit in the conference room can influence how receptive the client is to you and your ideas and ultimately how successful you are at winning new business.

CHANGE OF MINDSET

Let's say you invite me to a meeting. I ask, "What do we want to get out of this meeting? Do we want the client to agree to a certain trade or engagement? How are we going to know if this is a good meeting? Do we want another meeting? Do we want a meeting with this person's boss next time?"

A good meeting is not one in which the conversation is about news, weather, and sports. You have to think about exactly why you are having this meeting in order to plan for a worthwhile meeting. This sounds a little blunt, but it is a smart discipline to ask, "What do we want from this meeting?" In order to prepare for a good meeting, you have to know exactly what you want to accomplish.

You should always plan the first 25 words you want to say to open the meeting so that your meeting gets off to a strong start. I drive the people I work with crazy when I constantly tell them, "You cannot go into an important client meeting and talk about news, weather, and sports. You have to know your first three sentences." I have been to meetings with senior people who ask the client, "How are you doing?" or "What is new?" This is a weak approach, and it suggests that you put no preparation into the meeting.

If you know what your first 25 words are going to be, you might still be terrified, but you will not sound terrified. I have been known to record my first 25 words on my own voicemail and play them back to myself. Was I stuttering? Was I going too fast when I was speaking? Did the flow of the first 25 words work? Hearing myself say the first 25 words also helps to implant them in my head.

The best meetings are those that do not rely on a written presentation or book. Clients want advisers who listen, not human encyclopedias who try to rattle off every fact about the clients or their industry. If you have thought of better questions for the client, then you will have a better meeting. Listen to the client's answers to your questions. If you are a better listener, you will have better client meetings.

Just let the client talk, and do not interrupt. The more the client talks, the better he or she will think the meeting went.

HAVE A STRONG OPENING AND STRONG CLOSE

It is important that you have both a strong opening and a strong close to every client meeting. In addition to doing your research and practicing your opening, you need to be able to establish a rapport with the client, especially if it is a new client. This usually happens in the more casual conversations that occur before the official start of the meeting. You use your 25-word speech to open the official meeting, but you need an icebreaker to start conversation and to learn more about the client before the meeting actually begins.

I find that one of the most effective approaches is to ask the client, "How did you get started in the business?" Usually the client will be more than happy to tell you the story. That not only gets the client talking about himself or herself—always a positive thing—but it also often reveals areas of common ground between you and the client.

The benefit of asking that open-ended question is that you will find "clicks" with the client. These are moments when two people click or make an instant connection. Ori and Rom Brafman wrote a book about this phenomenon called *Click: The Forces Behind How We Fully Engage with People, Work, and Everything We Do.*[1] It is an investigation of the forces behind what makes us click with certain people. You will learn what you

[1]Ori Brafman and Rom Brafman, *Click: The Forces Behind How We Fully Engage with People, Work, and Everything We Do* (New York: Random House, 2010).

and the client have in common: You both like the NFL. You grew up in the same state. You went to the same school. Look for the clicks and draw the conversation to what you and the client have in common to cement the relationship with your client.

One simple but effective way to open the business part of the meeting is to reverify the question, using a foil if you can. In other words, state what you understand the client's need to be, and ask whether that is still the question the client wants you to answer in this meeting. A situation can change significantly in the weeks that you and your team have been preparing your presentation, so you need to make sure you have the latest information and use that information to tailor your presentation.

When we start the meeting, I might say to the client, "When we set up this meeting 10 days ago, the topic was ballpoint pens. My colleague was not on our call. For my colleague's benefit, would you please tell her a little bit more about why ballpoint pens are important in terms of your strategy and financial situation?" In this example, I am using my colleague as a foil, but for good reason. The whole question may have morphed, and we do not want an unproductive meeting. One of the worst things is to waste a client's time with a low-value meeting.

This approach gives the client the chance to say, "We no longer want to talk about ballpoint pens. We want to talk about wristwatches." Perhaps the client was not clear when the meeting was set up, perhaps you misunderstood, or perhaps the issue has changed. In any case, you now know what is important to the client right now, and you and your colleague can probably scramble and shift the presentation to an ad hoc discussion of wristwatches.

If the client confirms that the original question is still correct, then you present your analysis. Tell the client that you examined several strategic alternatives and you would like to propose the two most compelling alternatives, compare those alternatives, and help the client choose the best alternative.

It is important not to jump to the answer with the client. Walk the client through the alternatives, and present the alternatives in a balanced way.

A senior banker once told me to remember: "As compared to what?" I really did not understand what he meant. He said, "Well, the client has option X, with these plusses and minuses. Or, the client has option Y, with these plusses and minuses." You want to talk with the client in a very balanced way and say, "You can do option X, or you can do option Y."

Don't come down too strongly on the side of one alternative, such as recommending option X. If you were to say to the client, "Here are all the reasons you have to do X. Everybody is doing X," you come off as pushing a product rather than presenting options and then helping the client make the decision. As we discussed earlier, a long-term, client-centered approach helps to build strong client relationships, and that ultimately benefits your firm. You aren't just pushing a product; you want to help a client solve a problem.

You also need to think about what you hope to obtain by the end of the client meeting. You might want to get another meeting. You might want to get the client to share confidential information with you. You might want to get an introduction to the board of directors. You might want to get the client to agree to sign an engagement letter. Knowing where you want to go in the next step will help you get there.

A former senior banker once taught me a great way to close a client meeting: "Let me sum up. You know that we value our relationship with you. This meeting has been very valuable in terms of gaining a better understanding of the issues you are facing. As a result of this meeting, our understanding of your situation has improved significantly. I am highly confident that we will do a great job in helping you to solve this issue. I suggest that we meet again next Tuesday to follow up." Once you have gotten what you want, promptly leave the meeting.

HOW TO ASK FOR THE ORDER

This is the scariest part of the whole book: asking for business. I can tell you exactly where I was and how terrified I was the very first time it was up to me to ask a client for a big order. But it does not have to be as scary for you as I felt it was for me.

First, at the end of a client meeting you might say something like, "So let me sum up. We discussed why this issue is important and timely. We conducted analyses with your numbers and your staff. We compared several options, and we worked together to find the optimal solution. In my judgment, this is a compelling opportunity. Would you like to go forward so we can get to work?"

Then, stop talking and listen. One of two things is going happen. The client might say, "Done, yes." If that happens, thank him or her and leave the room or get off the phone.

Don't continue selling. For example, say I suggest to my wife that we should go to the movies this weekend. We discuss the options in the theater, and decide on a film. Then I continue to talk about the movie we chose, saying, "Let me tell you about the cinematography, let me tell you about the costumes, let me tell you about the reviews, and so on." My wife probably would say, "I already said yes—stop selling!"

If you continue selling after getting the order, you run the risk of saying something that causes the clients to change their mind or reduce the size of the engagement, which makes it less attractive to you.

What should you do if the client says no?

DEALING WITH REJECTION

> "You know what separates the great players from the average player? The average player always focuses on the last play. The great player always focuses on the next play. An average player misses a shot, okay, goes down and commits a stupid foul. A great player misses a shot, total erasure, then goes down and steals the ball and makes a layup."
>
> *Mike Krzyzewski, Hall of Fame college basketball coach*

When you are dealing with clients and asking for the order, you must learn how to deal with rejection when the client says no.

If the client says no, then you ask why. Your goal in asking why is to learn why the client turned down your offer. Most likely, the client has an objection to your solution, product, or service. Objections generally fall into one of several categories:

- No need right now
- No urgency right now
- Too expensive
- Wrong solution for my issue

However, this first objection might be the easy answer, rather than what is at the root of the rejection. The second objection is likely to be the most important. For example, the client might initially say, "It's too expensive." But that probably is not the real issue. If you ask, "What else don't you like about this proposal?" or, "Help me understand your concern," the client might say, "Oh, well, you know, it's pretty complicated. I don't think I can explain it to my boss." Now you have a better feel for what you need to do to address the client's objections. If you don't ask the second question about objections, you will not learn the real obstacle, and you will not have a chance to overcome or resolve it.

The best professional services people anticipate objections and rehearse their response. I would recommend having a colleague roleplay with you to consider potential client objections and rehearse how to manage those objections.

Rejection is inevitable when you are in the business of persuading clients to use your firm to find solutions to their problems. Dealing with rejection is a core skill. The most important part of your mindset is to avoid rejecting clients who are rejecting you. If you have bad chemistry with a client and you have tried to improve the relationship with no success, it may be time to raise your hand and ask the boss to take you off the client coverage team.

XIII

DIFFERENTIATING YOURSELF WITH CLIENTS

DIFFERENTIATING YOURSELF THROUGH LIKABILITY AND TRUST

The people who are real rainmakers in professional services have a few traits in common. They are smart enough but not always the smartest. They are hardworking enough but not always the hardest working. The key differentiators for bringing in new business are that their clients like and trust them and that they bring a unique insight.

In order to differentiate yourself, your clients have to trust you and believe that you are acting in their best interests rather than in your own. They cannot feel that you are suggesting a transaction or engagement that will benefit you more than them. You are engaged by a client to solve their problem and you can develop trust only if you deliver a result that they perceive is in their best interest.

Placing the client's interests first applies to any interaction you have with a client, whether it is directly transactional or not. One time I was flying on a private jet from Geneva to London with a very urbane CEO and his new wife. We were talking about which languages are spoken in Switzerland, and I noted that the Swiss speak German, French, and Italian. The CEO's wife asked, "When we get to London, will they speak English?"

I froze like a deer in the headlights. The CEO was staring daggers at me. I paused and then replied, "That is a great question. London is part of the United Kingdom. In Scotland, they speak Scottish Gaelic and English. In Ireland, they speak Irish Gaelic and English. In Wales, they speak Welsh. In London, they will speak English." The CEO looked very relieved and was happy with my answer because I did not embarrass his wife and I showed I had his best interests in mind.

Here is another example of putting the client's interests first by successfully managing a culturally sensitive interaction. I had a colleague, let's call him Richard. His parents were Chinese, but he spent his entire life in the United States. Richard worked in the New York office of Morgan Stanley and was transferred to our Hong Kong office. Richard was fluent in Mandarin and he understood the cultural nuances of doing business in Asia. In particular, Richard understood the importance of "saving face" in various parts of Asia. To lose face means to lose honor or dignity. Brutal honesty can cause offense, and the loss of face is especially upsetting or insulting in front of subordinates.

The scene was a private dining hall in a major Chinese city. A banquet was being held to thank and honor Richard for completing an important transaction. The client CEO was the host and was seated at Richard's immediate left. The host's subordinates filled the rest of the table. There was a menu printed in Mandarin showing the 10 courses that would be served. Course number five featured dog meat. Richard loved dogs and was horrified that he would have to eat dog meat. Richard was faced with a dilemma—insult the host by refusing the course made of dog meat or eating it. As the courses were served, Richard pondered his options. Richard quietly told the host he was honored by the sumptuous banquet but that he was born in 1970 under the sign of the dog. Therefore, the dog is sacred to him, and he could not eat dog. The host considered this for a moment and said that Richard could skip the dog course. Richard's quick thinking enabled him to diplomatically avoid a bad outcome.

People want to do business with people they like. It's important that you find ways to get people to like you, and placing the client's interests first is one of the most effective ways to do this.

The brass ring of client relationships is loyalty. A loyal customer is a repeat customer. Such a client will bring you opportunities to the exclusion of others and will come back after you make a misstep. Rapport is the foundation of trust, and trust, along with likeability and exceptional service, is the foundation of loyalty.

DIFFERENTIATING YOURSELF THROUGH INSIGHT

> "A moment's insight is sometimes worth a life's experience."
>
> *Oliver Wendell Holmes, Sr., American physician, poet, professor, lecturer, and author*

As I mentioned earlier, I have an old friend who would say, "A point of view is worth 20 IQ points." When you are working in professional services, you have to know what is going on in the world and how it affects your clients. If you are an officer of your firm and your client asks you something about a financial issue in the news, you can't say, "Well, wait a minute. I'll call a friend." You have to have a point of view.

Insight is a critical component of a point of view, and it also is a way of differentiating yourself with your clients. When I started out in investment banking, we were in the information and solutions business. We had access to the most up-to-date financial information via the broad tape ticker, a roll of paper connected to a Teletype machine that ticked along all day long—hence the term *ticker tape.*

Now everyone has access to that information immediately through electronic or digital media. Every CEO that I visit has not one but two Bloomberg screens in the office. As information has become commoditized, it is no longer enough to have access to information; now our value comes from the insight we can provide to clients. How do you differentiate yourself by turning *information* into *insight*?

Recently, I was talking to a major logistics company CEO about how sensitive his business model is to energy prices. If the price of crude oil jumped, I could call the CEO back with that information. But he probably would say, "Why are you wasting my time telling me this? I have my own Bloomberg, so tell me something I don't know."

Before you call your client, you need to turn that information into insight using a simple formula: Information plus context plus analysis plus judgment creates insight.

In this example, you have the information that the price of crude oil has increased significantly. You also have the context. Because you are a good listener, you know what your client is focused on and worried about. Now take the information and context and add the analysis and judgment—with a little help from your colleagues.

For example, I would call an analyst and ask her to change the price of crude oil in our financial model for the logistics company. Ten minutes later, when she has finished the new model, I know what the new crude oil price does to the logistics company's earnings, cash flow, balance sheet, and dividend.

Then I call several smart people at the firm to get their perspective and insights. I may call experts in equity capital markets, credit, mergers and acquisitions, commodities, and research to check their views on the pricing of crude oil and to gauge what they are telling their clients. That gives me a collective judgment, and prepares me to call the client. Now I can call the client and say, "I am sure that you have seen that crude oil has jumped to X. I remember the conversation we had the other day. We did some analysis on your business model, and we think that the sell side is going to say this, the rating agencies are going to say that, and your board of directors is going to be concerned about these things. We have two ideas for you. How about if we come visit you next Tuesday and talk about these ideas?"

This approach is much more likely to get you a meeting with the client. Not everyone uses this approach because it is harder to combine information, context, analysis, and judgment. You have to remember, we are not in the information business anymore. It used to be more important to be first with the information. Now it is important to be thoughtful with useful insight rather than first with information. Do the extra hard work to create insights and thereby differentiate yourself from the competition.

USING THE APPLE FIVE STEPS OF SERVICE

Did you know that there is actually a system for how Apple Store employees interact with customers? The Apple Store has developed a specific method of training called the Apple Five Steps of Service[1] to guide its employees in interacting with customers. Every Apple Store employee is trained to walk through the five steps in each and every transaction. The system is based on the acronym *APPLE* and includes these steps:

Approach customers with a personalized, friendly welcome. Customers' perceptions of their experience is formed in the first 10 seconds. Make the first impression count.

Probe politely to understand all the customer's needs. The Apple Store employee asks a series of closed- and open-ended questions to match the customer with the right product, not the most expensive product.

Present a solution for the customer to take home today. Apple likes to remind its store employees that they are not in the business of selling computers; they are in the business of "enriching lives." A sale isn't the only way to enrich the life of a customer and to build loyalty.

Listen for and resolve any issues or concerns. Customers have what are called "unexpressed" wishes or concerns. Specialists are trained to pick up on these concerns during the "probing" step, which is why it is important to ask good questions.

[1] Carmine Gallo, "Apple Store's Secret Sauce: 5 Steps of Service," *Forbes* (May, 16, 2012).

End with a fond farewell and an invitation to return. How people feel when they end a transaction significantly impacts how they perceive the brand and whether they are likely to recommend the brand to others.

These five steps of service can be applied to almost any client interaction, including professional services. If you can understand your clients' explicit and implicit needs and make them feel appreciated, your clients will reward you with wallet share and loyalty.

XIV

ASSESSING THE CLIENT SITUATION

KNOW YOUR CLIENT'S VITAL SIGNS

When you go for a physical, your doctor takes your vital signs, including temperature, blood pressure, respiration, and pulse. When you go to a client meeting, you should think about the client's vital signs. For example,

- How much business does that client have to award in the next 12 months?
    - Are there any elephant transactions (really large deals) on the horizon?
- Who are your competitors at this client?
    - How many competitors do business with this client?
    - Are those competitors as good or better than your firm?
    - Does this client have too many service providers?
    - Where do you rank among all of the firms that cover this client (e.g., are you fifth out of five firms)?

It is important to know where you stand with each of your clients and to know each client's potential future revenue. There are only so many hours in a day, so you have to invest your time in the clients with the highest probability for returns. Also, sooner or later, your management is going to ask you, "Where do we stand with that client?" You want to have an up-to-date view on your coverage strategy for each client and the rationale for that coverage strategy.

Some clients have what is called a rotation philosophy. They award transactions to all of the banks that cover them on a rotating basis. I have made the mistake of taking a co-manager spot in a dinky bond deal one week, only to have the same client announce a $50 billion mergers-and-acquisitions (M&A) trade the next week.

After the announcement, I said to the client, "Hey, that was our M&A idea." The client said, "That's true, but we just gave you that bond deal last week." If I had realized the client had a rotational strategy, I probably would have passed on the bond deal to be part of the M&A deal that was our idea in the first place.

To help you understand more about your client, you need to have a good friendly contact on the inside. An inside contact can provide great insights that are critical to understanding how to really make progress with a client. A client contact can help you understand the client's philosophy about awarding business and what is in the pipeline of business to be awarded by the client.

Say you worked really hard and lost the bake-off on a deal. If you have a good relationship, the client probably feels at least a little guilty about not giving you the business. You need to be resilient and not get angry and upset about missing that piece of business. If you know what is in the client's pipeline, you can play the guilt card and ask for the next desirable piece of business. Remember that guilt has a shelf life, so don't wait too long to use that card.

HOW TO KNOW IF YOU ARE MAKING PROGRESS WITH A CLIENT

The goal for a successful client relationship is to develop a progressively deeper connection with the client. It is important to periodically assess how strong your client relationship is and to continuously improve that relationship.

The best way to cover a client is to have multiple people from your professional services firm talking with multiple people at the client. Ideally, you want senior people on the client coverage team building relationships with the senior people at the client and its board of directors. Junior people at your firm should be actively covering junior people at the client. This is how you identify key client contacts and build relationships early in their careers.

Also, you want multiple subject matter experts at your firm building relationships with the product experts at the client. If the client is global, then coverage requires a global strategy and coordination. The entire coverage team should aim to deliver value to the client through differentiated content, providing context and networking opportunities. It requires multiple touchpoints and coordinated strategic efforts to effectively execute on multiple-point client coverage.

The key objective is to build a long-term client relationship. How do you know you are making progress with a client?

- If your client is sharing more confidential information with you, that is *good.*
- If your client says to you, "I have not talked to any other professional services firm, but I would love your thoughts," that is *better.*
- If your client says to you, "One of your competitors had this idea, which I would like to bounce off you," that is *great.*
- If your client asks for personal help like a job reference or a personal favor, that is *excellent* because it will create loyalty.
- If your client invites you and your spouse to a social event, that is a *wow* because it shows rapport and a personal affinity.

You should engage in periodic balance-of-trade conversations between the coverage team at your professional services firm and the client team. The goal is to establish a relationship that is equitable for both parties.

You need to realistically assess the strength of the client relationship after 6 months, 12 months, and 18 months. Are you doing free work for the client? Did you help the client get a board seat? If it has been 18 months and the client has handed out seven pieces of business and your firm has gotten the worst piece of business, then it is time for a balance-of-trade conversation with the client.

It is important to calmly have this conversation when you are not in the middle of making a deal. The conversation should recap what each party has brought to the relationship. At the end of that discussion, you should agree on what your firm should do more of or less of in the future and what you should get in return from the client.

XV

HOW FIRM STRATEGY IS COMMERCIAL

KNOW YOUR FIRM'S STRATEGY

The ability to formulate and implement business strategy is one of the most important enablers of sustained organizational success. Every professional services firm has a strategy. How are you going to get ahead at your firm? You need to know your firm's strategy and what it means for you and your clients in order to get ahead at your firm.

Professional services firms deploy business strategies to drive revenue growth, gain market share, generate productivity, respond to regulatory reform, manage risk, control costs, and maintain or restore trust and credibility. Those strategies usually contain the same basic elements: what we do, how we do it, and the results we would like to achieve for our shareholders and employees. The strategy for a professional services firm has to be dynamic. It continues to evolve because of competitive, regulatory, technological, and market changes. It is important to stay current on your firm's strategy.

Knowing the strategy is also a core part of your job as an officer of a professional services firm. If you run into a senior leader of your firm in the elevator, don't be surprised if the senior leader asks you about the firm's strategy. You might even want to take the opportunity to talk about how the strategy is working or what you are doing to help execute the strategy.

When you are talking with a client, you need to be articulate about your firm's strategy. Your clients need to understand that your firm's strategy puts the client's interests first and creates benefits for the client. This is how firm strategy is connected to commercial impact.

CONNECT FIRM STRATEGY TO COMMERCIAL IMPACT

A successful execution of the firm's strategy can improve the firm's financial performance, attract and retain top talent, and enhance the culture and values of your firm. Successfully executing the firm's strategy delivers commercial results and creates shareholder value as in Figure 15.1. Aligning strategy and execution can be a difficult task, but it is critical for achieving business results.

If your firm has developed a well-conceived strategy, then you should be executing more client engagements that serve the clients well. As a result,

Figure 15.1 Connect Firm Strategy to Commercial Impact

your firm will improve business results and generate more profit. Higher profit means your firm will be able to pay competitive compensation to its employees.

If your team is executing the firm's strategy, profitability is up, and compensation is competitive, then your ability to attract and retain employees should improve. Talent is a professional services firm's greatest asset, and keeping talent engaged is critical to the long-term success of your firm. Finally, the execution of the firm's strategy should be done in a manner that treats clients and employees in a way that is consistent with your firm's culture and values.

Understanding and executing the firm's strategy is the critical foundation to achieving commercial results.

CLIENTS HIRE YOUR FIRM AND THEY HIRE YOU

> "Your premium brand had better be delivering something special, or it's not going to get the business."
>
> *Warren Buffett, American businessman*

A professional services firm's brand represents something to a client that gives your firm an advantage over competitors in terms of preference and trust. In some respects, a brand conveys a promise of quality, credibility, and experience. Brands are valuable. Many companies put the value of their brand on their balance sheet.

The brand is valuable because it is an important element in differentiation. You know your firm has an effective brand when clients want to do business with your company. There is a greater need than ever for professional services firms to differentiate themselves, and the firm's brand is a key component of differentiation. If your firm does not have a *premium brand,* then you risk becoming a commodity service provider—and that means you must compete primarily on price.

The meltdown of 2008 was followed by an erosion of client loyalty and trust in professional services firms. As a result, banks, accounting, law, and consulting firms were being asked to cut fees or participate in fierce request for proposal (RFP) battles just to retain a relationship. A strong, differentiated brand is of great value in such a hypercompetitive environment. A brand can build and sustain goodwill to carry a professional services firm over rough patches. However, the brand equity of Arthur Young, Dewey and LeBouef, Lehman Brothers, and Bear Stearns—all eminent firms in their day—was not enough to save those firms from the collapse of their reputations and lack of access to capital.

There are times when a client can enhance its reputation or credibility by hiring a firm with a strong brand. Examples would be the lead underwriter on an IPO or a legal opinion from a highly regarded law firm in litigation or a critical regulatory matter.

However, all the recognition and awareness in the world will not overcome negative experiences that a client has with a service provider. Since client experiences almost always come from interactions with specific individuals within the firm, everyone inside the firm must understand and represent the values of the firm. In marketing terms, the process of creating a brand is called *building*—based on the image of constructing a structure from the foundation up. Building a brand can take years or decades, but you or your colleagues can damage it in a single day with a single interaction. Keep in mind that such damage can hurt your firm with stakeholders such as regulators, investors, and potential recruits.

A brand is an amalgamation of business strategy, leadership, culture and values, history and background, client perceptions, competitive context, and financial and strategic durability. At a time when the need to differentiate is more critical than ever, professional services firms often communicate very similar brand messages. A recent survey of brand attributes by DeSantis Breindel found that the most common words professional services firms used were:

- *Client-focused*
- *Global*
- *Service*

- *Relationships*
- *Trust*
- *Experience*
- *Results-driven*
- *Quality*
- *Integrity*

Many of these most common brand attributes do little to differentiate professional services firms. Nonetheless, it is unlikely that a CEO or CFO would hire a firm that was not focused on client needs or did not have integrity.

Consulting, banking, accounting, and legal firms believe that businesses hire the firm, not the team. Branding is not binary. The firm can have a successful brand, and so, too, can the individual employees/executives have their brands, relationships, and reputations. Hence, you need to be mindful of how much your personal relationships with clients can leverage your firm's brand.

The reality is that while prospective clients may shortlist a few firms, they do in fact hire the people on the team. Service buyers don't want a generic team. They want people who are experienced subject matter experts and industry experts for a particular project. Clients don't have the time or patience to serve as a training ground in order to make your team more capable for the next client's assignment. They want the best people for the task at hand now. Clients also have a strong preference for a team that includes someone senior they have met before the project starts.

It is important to keep perspective about the reasons that clients do business with your firm. Are the clients "your clients" or the "firm's clients"? When you hand out a business card or write a formal opinion, the name or logo of your firm is usually prominently displayed.

An important litmus test of the power of your firm's brand is how easily you are able to make a first appointment. The prospective client will be most receptive if you have been given a referral or if your firm has a strong brand.

TRUST-BASED CLIENT RELATIONSHIPS

> "Spend a lot of time talking to customers face to face. You'd be amazed how many companies don't listen to their customers."
>
> *Ross Perot, American businessman*

> "The ability to establish, grow, extend and restore trust is the key professional and personal competency of our time."
>
> *Stephen M. R. Covey, American writer*

Just as we discussed a magic formula for career advancement (ability, opportunity, courage), there is a winning formula for creating and maintaining client relationships. The magic words are *know, like, trust.*

This process involves getting to know your prospective client, increasing your likability factor, and building trust. Getting to know potential clients requires face-to-face meetings. As discussed earlier, being part of a firm with a strong brand not only facilitates obtaining meeting appointments but more importantly can jumpstart this winning formula, especially the *know* and *trust* aspects.

The simplest way to get to know people is to listen to them carefully and find ways to add value before you ever try to sell them something. The more someone likes you, the more they begin to trust you. The goal is to create a relationship of "subject matter expert and interested party" rather than seller and buyer. A lawyer from a national law firm and I were once advising a client on a major project, and the lawyer said to the client, "You have a big problem, but you are in good hands with Runde and me."

A common mistake professional services people make is to jump straight to the subject matter expert role rather than go through the more deliberate process of know, like, trust. Another error is to be pushy, causing the client to feel you are selling a product rather than serving as a trusted adviser. The more someone trusts you, the more they share their personal concerns and needs with you.

To be clear, no amount of personal connection can substitute for exceptional service and work product. Exceptional service includes knowing the client's company, strategy, competitors, and customers. Respond promptly to phone calls and emails. Some bankers worry about finding the right answer first, while I prefer to answer an email right away by replying "checking" and then try to sort out a thoughtful response. A phone call beats an email every time when you are trying to build a client relationship, because it is real-time and more interactive and personal.

Another hallmark of excellent service is to summarize a meeting in terms of next steps and timelines. Just as asking senior people about deadlines is a best practice when you are starting out in your career, asking clients at the end of a meeting about the deadlines for a project can prevent frustration and chaos.

When you meet with your customers and encourage them to talk to you, you should speak only to break the ice and get them comfortable, and then only to ask questions. The rest of the time, stay quiet and listen. Ideally, you also will spend a lot of time just watching. There are times when bringing a colleague to a client meeting can be enlightening. While your colleague is talking, watch everyone else in the room for their reactions. A nod of approval, a roll of the eyes, or a deep breath can all mean different things—and it's worth asking that person later about his or her reaction.

I learned a valuable lesson about earning client trust after working on a project for many months. It involved a merger of two large railroads, and at the time it would have been the biggest transaction of my career. Our team consisted of several junior professionals, a very senior partner, and me.

The scene was a New York hotel where we had booked three separate, small meeting rooms. The first room was for our client with the Morgan Stanley team and the client's legal advisers. The second room was a neutral negotiating room. The third room was for the other railroad company and its advisers. We will call the CEO of our client Tom.

Although the bidding had gone back and forth for about 10 days, it was clear that this particular evening was going to be the "make or break" moment. Our analysis indicated that an offer price for the other railroad of $34 per share was excellent value for our client and represented about a 35 percent premium over the other company's current stock price. We took

Tom through our thinking in terms of strategic benefits, shareholder value creation, and other financial data one last time. Tom told us he had what he needed and left our room to meet alone with the CEO of the other railroad. After about 15 minutes, Tom came back to our room and said he had offered $34 per share and the other CEO made a counter proposal of $36 per share. Tom asked our senior partner what he should do.

We told Tom that our Morgan Stanley team needed to caucus to discuss the current offer on the table. We all agreed that our client was getting close to the valuation limit and that our senior partner should tell Tom that he should be prepared to walk away from this transaction, even though we knew it would have been easier to say, "Sure, what's a few dollars more?" Our senior partner went back to Tom and told him our collective advice that he should be willing to walk away from the deal if the price got too high.

Tom said, "I knew I could trust you guys. Can you give my board a fairness opinion at $35 per share?" All eyes were on me. I passed around our valuation materials again, and it showed we could give a fairness opinion up to about $37 per share. Tom thanked us and went back to the neutral room one last time. A few minutes later, he came back and told us he had a deal at $34.50 per share.

Not only did we represent Tom that night, but for years later he was a very loyal client—all because our senior partner said he should be prepared to walk away from the deal. Tom knew that he could trust us to put his interests ahead of our interests. That was the night I learned that know, like, and trust are the foundation of high-quality, long-term client relationships.

3

BECOMING AN EXCEPTIONAL LEADER

XVI

ENGAGING AND LEADING PEOPLE

"You manage things; you lead people"

Grace Hopper, Admiral U.S. Navy

Part 2 of this book provides strategies for covering clients and building trust with your clients. As a leader in a professional services firm, you face completely different issues than you do in covering clients. In this section, I want to share with you some of the things I have learned about leadership.

I grew up in Wisconsin, where both of my grandfathers were dairy farmers. When you are a farmer, you manage a herd of cattle or a corn crop. Farmers earn money and are responsible stewards of the land. Running a successful dairy farm requires optimizing the available resources—land, livestock, labor, and capital. Said differently, cows and crops need to be managed. You need to tightly manage the farm in order to deliver goods and earn a living.

Business has changed a lot since my grandfathers ran their dairy farms, and professional services firms are very different from dairy farms. Today, we have employees who have high degrees of specialized expertise, education, and/or experience. Their work is based on their intellect in a business environment that is global, complex, and technology-driven.

The late management expert Peter Drucker was one of the first to recognize the importance of knowledge workers. He predicted that they would change the way businesses were structured. When dealing with the knowledge worker, "one does not 'manage' people," Drucker wrote. "The task is to lead people. And the goal is to make productive the specific strengths and knowledge of every individual."[1]

A professional services employee needs to be led and engaged, not just managed. If we want to motivate people, we must give them opportunities to build, innovate, and create. We need to provide leadership and understand the difference between a good leader and a good manager.

A good manager is an operational expert with the authority to instruct a group of people to complete tasks and achieve the organization's goals. If I visited the multibillion-dollar construction project, I could find many excellent project managers. They assemble teams, assign deliverables, and hold team members accountable for meeting deadlines. These individuals would have subject matter expertise and deliver the project on time and on budget. They would be focused on the "here and now."

But are good managers necessarily good leaders? Do they know how to motivate their employees and keep them engaged? Managers plan, organize, and coordinate; leaders inspire and motivate.

It can be hard to find good leaders in professional services firms, which generally reward and promote top producers for their performance as individual contributors. But if you are a top producer, that does not mean that you will be a good leader.

This is the Peter Principle at work. The Peter Principle is a management theory developed by Laurence J. Peter that says that the selection of people for a position is based on their performance in their current role, rather than

[1] Peter Drucker, *Management Challenges for the 21st Century* (New York: Harper Collins, 2001), pp. 21–22.

on their ability to succeed in their next role.[2] The Peter Principle is based on the notion that employees get promoted as long as they are competent at their jobs, but at some point a job becomes too challenging, so they fail to be promoted beyond that job. In other words, employees rise to their level of incompetence and stay there. Taken to the extreme, this could mean that every leadership position in a company would be filled with people who are incompetent leaders even though they are big producers. Therefore potential leaders need to be scrutinized for their people skills more than their technical or tactical deal skills.

What does it take to pivot from being great working with clients to being a great leader? You need to learn to delegate work and not micromanage your team. The day-to-day leader of the coverage team has to be able to manage the client relationship, have the day-to-day responsibilities for the team, and get the credit for client wins. As a more senior leader, you are there to protect and support the team, but not to impede its progress.

Many executives have worked hard for years to reach the upper levels of management, but only a select few will ever reach the top of the ladder. *What Got You Here Won't Get You There*, a best-selling book by Marshall Goldsmith and Mark Reiter,[3] discusses how to make this transition and offers guidelines to help eliminate work habits that may be holding you back from where you want to go.

What will get you to the top of the ladder at your professional services firm? As we said earlier, most professional services firms have published the performance evaluation criteria by level. Your firm will have different performance evaluation forms for a vice president and above versus an associate. There are reasons for differences in those performance evaluation forms.

As you become more senior at your firm, you need to move away from being an individual contributor who just covers clients to being a team leader. As your leadership responsibilities increase, it is not advisable to try

[2]Laurence J. Peter, *The Peter Principle* (New York: Bantam Books, 1972).
[3]Marshall Goldsmith and Mark Reiter, *What Got You Here Won't Get You There* (New York: Hyperion, 2007).

to do all of the client work yourself. The business is too specialized, too complicated, and too global. It is too complex to understand the subtleties of all of the different industry verticals. For example, if you are a banker covering the transportation industry, you can't be a deep-subject-matter expert in both railroad companies and airlines. If you cover the healthcare industry, you can't be a deep-subject-matter expert in the pharmaceutical industry and the healthcare services industry.

It is very difficult to be up to speed on what is happening in Frankfurt as well as in Hong Kong unless you have an industry-leading global team around you. Today, there are different functions and different product specialists you need to support your client coverage. In order to be an effective leader, you need to build a global team of industry and product experts who can each pitch in to support you and your clients.

THREE HATS

> "It is a terrible thing to look over your shoulder when you are trying to lead—and find no one there."
>
> *Franklin D. Roosevelt, United States president*

Every day when you come to work, you are wearing three hats: You have to conduct your regular job responsibilities, you have to manage, and you have to lead.

Command and control works very well in the military. When I was in the Navy, the commanding officer and the chain of command were clearly codified. You knew who had the authority to direct each layer of people to achieve a mission or goal. As a young naval officer, I remember postings all around the ship that clearly stated the admiral, vice admirals, rear admirals, commodores, captains, and commanders. Command-and-control management works well with a highly structured organization with clearly defined tasks, like the military.

But the private-sector workforce has evolved. We now have multiple generations in the workforce. We have increased diversity in the workforce.

Expectations have changed. As a result, you must learn when to wear each of your three hats:

1. *You have a day job.* In your day job, you execute your firm's strategy, and you are commercial and turn relationships into revenue. In Part 2 of this book, we talked about how it is important to know your firm's strategy and what it means for you and your team. You also need to build client relationships and convert those client relationships into revenue for the firm.
2. *You have a management job.* As a manager, you are planning, organizing, and coordinating the tasks at hand. Your management job is the "here and now." You are planning your business by assigning tasks and establishing steps and timetables for achieving goals. You are allocating resources to achieve those goals. You are delegating work and guiding your team. You are creating budgets and reporting on your financial and business results. You are holding team members accountable. You are filling out and giving performance evaluations.
3. *You have a leadership job.* As a leader, you define a clear direction for the future of the business. Communication is a differentiator for leaders. You communicate the strategy so that it is understandable to everyone on the team. You leverage your experience and communication skills to make complex issues, conflicts, products, or coverage strategies simple to understand. You create alignment by working with others to create the conditions for success. When necessary, you influence and move others to act. You serve as a role model. You motivate and inspire individuals and teams. You encourage people to overcome project and career barriers (political, bureaucratic, skill, support) and encourage people to take calculated career risks.

As a leader, you bring out the best in people by understanding their skills and abilities and encouraging them to reach their full potential. I have a friend who likes to say, "The best test of leadership is followership." Followership is a practical metric of your ability to lead.

An exceptional leader is aware that team members become followers for different reasons. Some team members take direction because you are the boss. Others follow you because of what you can and have accomplished. Another group follows you because of what you can and have done for them personally or for the firm.

Integrity, clear communication, and optimism are the necessary ingredients for creating followers. Team members are very observant of how leaders conduct themselves, support or criticize senior management, and balance work and personal life. Leading by example is much more powerful than leading by words alone.

An inspiring leader uses effective communication to identify and simply describe a major goal or vision (i.e., market share, elephant deal, improved quality). The goal should clearly describe a destination that is distinctly different from where the team is now. The leader should have a plan for moving the team from where it is now to the destination. Milestones and time frames should be articulated at the beginning so that the team knows what is expected and how to see if the necessary progress is being made. The plan must be implemented with accountability. The leader should be able to explain the plan in understandable but energetic language. I have learned that if you give people perspective and context on why you are asking for something, rather than just telling them what you want, they will make better choices. The team should receive periodic updates from the leader as plans change or progress is made.

Team members are closely watching the leader for the ability to spot and develop talent. My own bias in selecting team members is that a positive attitude is more important than experience. I have had much greater success coaching and teaching enthusiastic younger people than trying to overcome attitudes of cynicism in jaded veterans.

Each of these three roles (day job, manager, and leader) is unique, and each requires a different mindset. You must understand the differences among these roles, determine which role is most appropriate based on the situation, and transition between the roles, if necessary. This requires self-awareness and practice on your part, but it is a skill well worth developing.

THREE Cs OF TEAM BUILDING

> "Coming together is a beginning. Keeping together is progress. Working together is success."
>
> *Henry Ford, American industrialist*

When you are wearing your team leader hat, how do you think about building the right team? In order to be an effective leader, you need to build the right team. I approach team building in terms of the three *C*s: composition, chemistry, and continuity.

First, let's talk about *composition.* You do not want all the people on your team to have the same skills, no matter how great those skills are. For example, if you are putting together a baseball team, you don't want to have all shortstops. You need to consider the overall mix of characteristics among the people on the team. You want people with different skills, expertise, and experience. The best leaders are aware of their own weaknesses, so they include on the team people who are strong in areas where they are not as strong. If you want to win, you need to have a diverse team of people with the right mix of skills, expertise, and experience to get the job done.

The next consideration is *chemistry*, which is the relationship among team members. A team with good chemistry works well together with limited conflict, is collegial, and achieves superior results. A team with proper chemistry tends to achieve higher levels of productivity because it spends less time disagreeing and more time solving problems. Such a team has members who think in terms of group success, not achieving individual goals. As professional services firms rely more and more on collaborative efforts, team leaders need to invest in understanding the basics of team chemistry. Chemistry, like culture, is highly influenced by leaders. Team members will tend to treat each other as you treat them.

Sometimes a leader must deal with toxic team members and their harmful behavior. If unaddressed, negativity spreads like a virus. I have seen resentful, selfish, or negative teammates cause low morale, upset clients, and even cause staff departures. Handling dysfunctional workers is difficult for me, so I learned to avoid hiring them in the first place by careful screening. If a problem developed later, my approach was to speak with them privately about specific examples of their disruptive actions and, when necessary, seek advice from a manager or a mentor or get assistance from human resources.

The final issue is *continuity*. In professional services, clients hate turnover. A team that has been together for a long time is a higher-functioning team. Team continuity helps to create a stronger work environment. Team members come to understand and trust one another better, and that can lead to a more cohesive team. Team members become personally engaged in the work and invested in the client; they are committed to working collaboratively to achieve a successful outcome for the client.

In professional services, discontinuity creates problems for the team and the clients. First, when someone leaves a firm, it hurts team morale, dynamics, and productivity. Second, discontinuity upsets the client, who may have shared confidential information with the person who left the firm. Finally, the person who leaves may go to a competitor, creating rivalry for the client team at the former firm.

A team leader needs to carefully monitor these three *C*s: composition, chemistry, and continuity.

SCREENING PROSPECTIVE TEAM MEMBERS

"Life is too short to hang out with people who aren't resourceful."

Jeff Bezos, American technology entrepreneur and investor

The first step in building the right team is screening prospective team members for the attributes you are looking for on your team. Some team leaders do not ask the best interview questions or probe deeply enough to get the right information from an interviewee. These team leaders ask typical interview questions such as:

- What is your greatest weakness?
- How would you describe yourself?
- Why should we hire you?
- Why do you want to work here?

I have a different interview strategy that has worked well for me throughout my career. I ask targeted questions that help me determine if an applicant has the particular attributes that I believe are important to building an effective team. During interviews of prospective employees, I have always asked them about team sports they played and job experience.

First, I ask interviewees about their team sports experience, including basketball, field hockey, lacrosse, and softball. If the candidate did not play team sports, I ask about other group experiences like student government, debate team, theater groups, or music ensembles. I have found that these group experiences teach values that are important in the workplace, like teamwork, time management, shared goals, decision-making under pressure, and leadership.

Second, I ask about the interviewee's job experience. I learned a great deal from a range of part-time jobs that I held between the ages of 12 and 22. During that time, I worked in newspaper delivery and sales, and as a shelf stocker at a variety store, latrine cleaner and bed maker at a military post, disc jockey, radio announcer, factory janitor, factory chemist, and cucumber packer at a pickle factory. By working these entry-level jobs, I learned humility and gained a deep appreciation for the hard work required to be successful. These work experiences provided me with motivation to pursue higher education and made me grateful for the education that allowed me to pursue my banking career.

In the interview, I ask if the interviewee worked part time during high school and/or college. Holding a part-time job while pursuing a degree is hard work and shows a high level of personal responsibility. Students who work during their high school and/or college careers often have better time-management skills because they had to balance their work and studies. They gain valuable workplace experience in things like showing up on time and behaving appropriately. Students who work typically learn money management. Paychecks from a third party impact a young person more strongly than allowance from parents. Jobs can provide references for higher education applications.

It is my judgment that summer jobs show important character traits in the interviewee and teach the interviewee valuable skills and lessons not usually available in the classroom. These skills include:

- Searching for a job
- Taking an interview
- Dealing with a boss
- Dealing with customers and co-workers
- Building self-confidence

My screening questions are designed to discern if a candidate is entitled, jaded, or self-absorbed. I have found that the best teammates demonstrate they are able to work toward a common goal, are dependable and resourceful, and, when necessary, are willing to do what it takes in order to get the job done.

I have concluded that resourcefulness has its basis in ambition. Ambition helps one navigate and overcome the obstacles of life, to persist rather than to quit, and to find other ways to succeed when things get difficult or uncertain.

Here is an example of resourcefulness from my own experience. When I was 29, I was assigned to a financing for a very large U.S. industrial company. It was the biggest convertible bond offering in history at that time. We arranged a roadshow for the top executives of the client to visit large institutional investors around the United States and Europe. I was so excited that I bought a new pair of shoes to wear on the trip.

To set the scene, my boss and I were flying from New York to Houston with the senior client executives on the client's Gulfstream jet. As we landed in Houston, I looked out the window and saw the darkest storm clouds that I had ever seen. We landed at about 3:15 p.m., and the deluge began just as we got in the limousines.

We were hosting a reception for investors in downtown Houston at 5 p.m. The drive downtown usually takes about 30 minutes. By 4:30 p.m., the freeway traffic was not moving and we were only halfway there. We were worried that if we were late for the reception, the investors would go home and the trip would be a waste of time. The driver turned on the local radio news station that reported severe flash flooding in the Houston metro area. The reporter said water runoff was filling the streets and freeway underpasses, causing severe traffic jams as well as electrical outages and phone problems (mobile phones did not exist yet). The reporter also said residents should be aware that venomous copperheads were being flushed out of their dens.

My boss spotted a gas station that had pay phones about 50 yards across a flooded field. He told me to run across the field and call the hotel. I jumped out of the limo and realized that the water was about 12 inches deep. My first thought was that my new shoes were going to be ruined. My second thought was: copperheads! I covered those 50 yards in record time.

When I got to the gas station, there were five people waiting to use a pay phone. I asked why no one was using the other two pay phones, and I was told the phones in the area were going out of service and those two phones had just failed. I was desperate to use the one working phone. I started at the back of the line and offered each person five dollars to cut ahead of them. Four of the five people in line gladly accepted, and I soon got on the phone, called the hotel and spoke with the concierge. I begged him to open the bar, serve free drinks, offer the investors appetizers, and do anything else he could to keep the crowd in the reception room until we arrived.

I quickly waded back to the car. We arrived at the hotel at 5:25 p.m. and found a big crowd of happy investors still waiting for us. The client said to my boss, "Runde saved the day!" My boss was pleased. More than anything, I was relieved.

Resourcefulness, in my view, is one of the most desirable employee attributes.

XVII

THE WAR FOR TALENT

In the late 1990s, McKinsey & Company warned about the war for talent. It highlighted the coming talent shortage and encouraged companies to prioritize talent strategies around recruiting, retaining, and developing key employees.

Today, the talent shortage continues. I have found that most professional services firm CEOs are concerned about attracting and retaining the best talent.

If you were a CEO and I were your strategic consultant, my first three questions to you would be:

- Are you financially constrained?
- Are you opportunity constrained?
- Are you talent constrained?

Right after the 2008 financial crisis, most CEOs of professional services firms would have responded to those questions by saying that they were financially constrained, but today they are talent constrained. As the global economy picks up, CEOs are increasingly concerned about attracting and retaining the best talent.

The shortage is not just talent, but the right talent with the right mindset. The right talent has the proven ability to network, create trust-based client relationships, embrace teamwork and a diverse perspective, lead people, internalize the firm's strategy and culture, and deliver commercial results.

How can professional services firms compete effectively in this new war for talent? Leaders need to be strategic about talent and focus on a holistic talent approach, including recruitment, engagement, retention, mobility, and diversity.

- *Recruitment:* The top firms have a bigger pool of job candidates because they have a stronger employment brand. The employment brand describes a firm's reputation in the external market as an employer and a place to work, as opposed to the general corporate brand reputation. It takes a great deal of effort to build a firm's employment brand. Your firm's ability to recruit is directly dependent on your firm's engagement and retention strategy as well as financial results. Candidates are far more likely to trust a firm based on what its current and former employees have to say on social media than on its recruitment advertising.
- *Engagement:* Leaders know that innovation, productivity, and retention are much better if the workforce is engaged. Firms with high employee engagement clearly communicate the firm's business objectives and strategy through multiple channels. Performance metrics are clearly tied to business objectives and strategy. Engagement improves when employees are encouraged to work independently and creatively to solve problems. Rewarding top performers for taking responsibility also enhances engagement.
- *Retention:* Employee turnover is expensive, and it has a negative effect on company morale and recruiting. Positive, motivated, long-tenured employees are generally more productive and create more value than new hires. Employee retention strategies

can keep key employees at your firm while maintaining job performance and productivity. Many employers believe that retention is based on compensation, but the drivers of retention are the actions and attitudes that make employees feel successful, secure, and appreciated. Employees have a deep desire to feel that they are succeeding and that their talents and capabilities make a difference to the firm. It is also important to communicate to employees and reaffirm that their workplace contributions are having a positive impact. If you demonstrate loyalty to your employees, they will reciprocate with commitment and loyalty to the firm.

- *Mobility:* Employers need to provide internal mobility and career growth within the firm. Internal mobility is a dynamic internal process for developing and moving talent from role to role. To achieve internal mobility, firms should adopt the principles of talent planning at all ranks. Firms should provide transparent discussion of skills and potential and provide access to open internal positions.
- *Diversity:* It is important to attract, retain, and develop diverse professionals to spur innovation, drive growth, and sustain competitive advantage in the marketplace. Earlier in this book, I discussed how in my experience, a team beats an individual every time. Groups of people usually come up with better suggestions than an elite few. A team made up of members with different experiences, different perspectives, and different skills will come up with better answers. Effective integration of diverse teammates is smart business and creates a winning edge.

THE THREE *M*s

The Deloitte Millennial Survey about the needs and wishes of younger people in the workplace can be summarized in three *M* words: *meritocracy,*

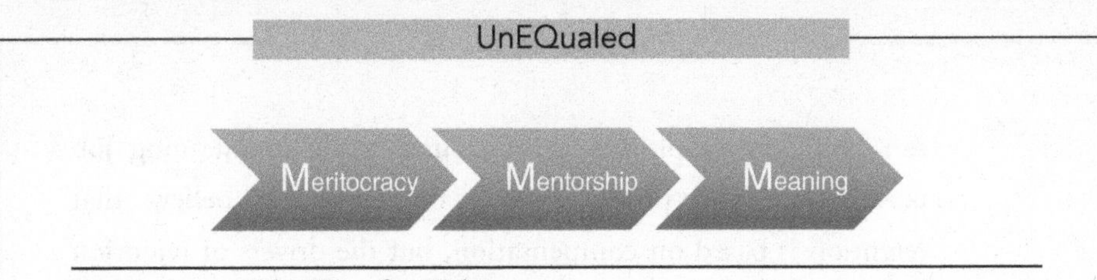

Figure 17.1 The War for Talent

mentorship, and *meaning* as seen in Figure 17.1.[1, 2] Modern leaders need to be aware of these needs and change their leadership mindset in order to recruit, develop, and retain this important pool of talent.

- *Meritocracy:* Millennials are attracted to teams and firms that reward their skills and contributions. Younger professionals want their ideas to be heard irrespective of their seniority. They are looking for transparent expectations and performance measurement that is based on objective value added rather than which school one attended or family background. In order to engage and motivate this group, a leader must show fairness and equality in considering younger people for new leadership positions.
- *Mentorship:* Gen X and especially millennials are motivated by continuous feedback and are inspired by periodic coaching and teaching. Young professionals are very eager to be involved in reverse mentoring. They love to show their tech savvy in a way that makes their boss more productive and up to date by teaching the boss about new applications and hardware.
- *Meaning:* The Deloitte study underscores the widely reported importance that young professionals attach to meaningful work. This cohort views work as a thing to do rather than a place to be. They want to understand the importance of doing a particular

[1]Alison Hillhouse, "Consumer Insights: MTV's 'No Collar Workers," Viacom (October 4, 2012), http://blog.viacom.com/2012/10/consumer-insights-mtvs-no-collar-workers/.

[2]Deloitte, "The 2016 Millennial Survey: Winning over the Next Generation of Leaders," http://www2.deloitte.com/content/dam/Deloitte/global/Documents/About-Deloitte/gx-millenial-survey-2016-exec-summary.pdf.

task. They hope to have a deep connection to their colleagues almost to the extent of creating a second family. They are highly motivated when they perceive their job and company are making a difference to society in terms of innovation or sustainability.

Many younger workers are asking themselves, "Why am I here, and why should I stay?" The most effective leaders will help them answer this question in a positive fashion by listening, being flexible, showing respect, and balancing autonomy with collaboration.

BE ALERT TO THE THREE *D*s

Today's leaders must show skill and adaptability in dealing with a perfect storm of talent issues:

- *Demographic turnover and variations in the workforce:* Today's workplace is multigenerational with millennials, generation X, and baby boomers. There are stark differences in the values, communication styles, and work habits of each generation. Baby boomers who have had their focus on having a career at one company are beginning to retire. Tech-savvy, younger employees are comfortable with a career working with multiple employers. Younger employees want to co-create rather than be part of a command-and-control chain. Also, understanding the purpose of their work and how that work fits into the bigger picture is critical to satisfaction. Leaders need to provide each employee with experience and opportunities that appeal to them as individuals. This requires leaders to be aware of their individual needs, preferences, and work styles.
- *Digital and mobile:* The digital revolution is transforming the way that you work. Technology allows you to work remotely anywhere and anytime, and to communicate and make decisions faster. Employees, clients, and customers are engaged via social media. In order to meet today's digital and mobile challenges,

leaders need to embrace and enable new ways of working using technology to improve the way the team works, boost employee productivity, and streamline collaboration.

- *Different markets and cultures:* Business is becoming increasingly global and interconnected. In several new business markets, such as China and India, the language, customs, and decision-making norms are unfamiliar to many Western players. Culture profoundly influences how people think, communicate, and behave. Understanding cultural differences and overcoming language barriers are critical to working with people of different cultures. There may be differences in communication style, mannerisms, and gestures.

Culture also affects the kinds of transactions business partners are willing to engage in and the way they negotiate those transactions. According to Gayle Cotton in her book, *Say Anything to Anyone, Anywhere: 5 Keys to Successful Cross-Cultural Communication*, there are important guidelines to facilitate multicultural communication and avoid confusion and conflict.[3]

1. *Create proactive cross-cultural communication.* You should be proactive rather than reactive in your interpersonal, phone, and email communications.
2. *Establish rapport to bridge the cultural gap.* By creating rapport with someone new, you establish a connection of trust and begin to build a relationship that bridges the cultural gap.
3. *Organize productive interactions.* Be aware of cultural sensitivities to avoid conflict when organizing multicultural interactions. For example, understand time differences and how different cultures relate to time.

[3]Gayle Cotton, *Say Anything to Anyone, Anywhere: 5 Keys to Successful Cross-Cultural Communication* (Hoboken, NJ: John Wiley & Sons, 2013).

4. *Pursue strategies for building strong relationships.* Understand cultural beliefs, values, and rules in order to build strong relationships.
5. *Recognize that success leaves clues.* Know the dos and don'ts for successful multicultural business and social interactions.

VALUES AND CULTURE

> "If you fail to honor your people, They will fail to honor you;
> It is said of a good leader that When the work is done, the aim fulfilled, The people will say, 'We did this ourselves.'"
>
> *Lao Tzu, 604–531 B.C., founder of Taoism*

Culture is unique for every organization, and it is one of the hardest things to change. Culture creates and demonstrates the values of the professional and social environment of the firm. It is mostly unwritten and has been developed over time. In his book, *What It Takes: Seven Secrets of Success from the World's Greatest Professional Firms*, Charles Ellis explains how cultural characteristics such as innovation and a commitment to excellence can drive organizational success.[4]

Organizational culture is a critical factor in the success of your firm. If you want to thrive as a leader in your firm, you need to understand your firm's organizational culture.

Organizational culture manifests itself in:

- How the firm treats clients, employees, and other stakeholders
- How decisions are made, including the role of consensus building
- How information and influence are shared
- How zealous employees are in terms of pursuing the firm's strategy and goals while carefully adhering to ethics and compliance

[4]Charles Ellis, *What It Takes: Seven Secrets of Success from the World's Greatest Professional Firms* (Hoboken, NJ: John Wiley & Sons, 2013).

Morgan Stanley's culture includes putting clients first, integrity, and collegiality. It is important to remember that culture and values are strategic and commercial. In fact, a recent survey of business leaders by Bain & Company found that culture was regarded as just as important as strategy.

Character and culture of the firm are largely determined by the intentional actions of senior leaders. In professional services firms, senior people become role models for others because their actions carry the weight of their authority within the organization. Those leaders can improve retention and morale at their firms if they demonstrate strong cultural values because people aspire to be like them. In some cases, as people become more senior, they become overly dictatorial and uncompromising. Retention and morale suffer at their firm because of this discouraging atmosphere. Leaders must not overlook how social media can make each company's culture publicly known in a manner that affects recruiting and retention.

Once a firm has established a cooperative and supportive culture, it is important to recruit new talent who embrace the culture. Team members recognize and understand the culture based on such factors as behavior, engagement, recognition, and compensation.

XVIII

IMPORTANCE OF EXCEPTIONAL LEADERSHIP

HERZBERG'S MOTIVATION-HYGIENE THEORY

In the 1950s and 1960s, psychologist Fredrick Herzberg sought to understand employee satisfaction by asking people what they wanted from their jobs. He asked people to describe situations in which they felt really good and really bad about their jobs.

These results became known as Herzberg's Motivation-Hygiene Theory (also known as Herzberg's Two-Factor Theory). Herzberg's findings revealed that certain characteristics of a job are consistently related to job satisfaction while different factors are associated with job dissatisfaction (see Table 18.1).

The characteristics associated with job dissatisfaction are called *hygiene factors.* When these have been adequately addressed, people will not be dissatisfied. (Notice the double negative, "not dissatisfied.") Herzberg

Table 18.1 Herzberg's Factors for Satisfaction and Dissatisfaction

Factors for Satisfaction	Factors for Dissatisfaction
Achievement	Company policies
Recognition	Supervision
The work itself	Relationship with supervisor and peers
Responsibility	Work conditions
Advancement	Salary
Growth	Status
	Security

Source: Frederick Herzberg, "One More Time: How Do You Motivate Employees?" *Harvard Business Review* (January 2003).

acknowledged the complexity of the salary issue (money, earnings, etc.) and concluded that money is not a motivator in the same way as the primary motivators such as achievement and recognition.

If you want to motivate or engage your team, you have to focus on satisfaction factors like achievement, recognition, and responsibility that improve "happiness" with the job. As you evaluate your current job and Herzberg's Motivation-Hygiene Theory, who has the most direct impact on your achievement, recognition, and responsibility? Your immediate boss!

There is another way to look at the two columns of Herzberg's Motivation-Hygiene Theory. Herzberg said, "Job satisfiers deal with the factors involved in doing the job, whereas job dissatisfiers deal with the factors which define the job context." Job satisfaction factors are created by your immediate boss, so they are "micro" factors. Those "micro" factors are those on the left-hand side of the Herzberg chart shown in Table 18.1. Job dissatisfaction factors are generally top down or created by the C-suite at a professional services firm, so they are "macro." It is the micro factors that create growth and engagement in your job.

A TEAM NEVER FORGETS HOW YOU MAKE THEM FEEL

> "Appreciate everything your associates do for the business. Nothing else can substitute for a few well-chosen, well-timed, sincere words of praise. They're absolutely free and worth a fortune."
>
> *Sam Walton, American business man and entrepreneur*

> "If you treat an individual as he is, he will remain how he is. But if you treat him as if he were what he ought to be and could be, he will become what he ought to be and could be."
>
> *Johann Wolfgang von Goethe, German writer*

If you are going be an exceptional boss, you have to convince the people who work for you and with you that they can have faith in you and believe in you. I have learned that a team forgets what you said. A team forgets what you did. A team never forgets how you made them feel.

The only way that I could afford to go to college was through the Navy Reserve Officers Training Corps (ROTC) program. As a junior in college, I took a course called Naval Leadership. On the first day of class, the lieutenant commander came into the classroom and said, "If you only remember one thing about this whole course, remember to praise in public, criticize in private." I thought that would be something I would need to know in the Navy, with its command-and-control management style, but not in professional services.

When I was a junior person just starting out at Morgan Stanley, a very senior person was running the Investment Banking division. One day that senior person walked in to my bullpen, and in front of everyone he said, "Hey, Runde, you did a super job on that project." I had never thought about that before, but one pat on the back in front of the bullpen, and I was energized enough to go another 10,000 miles for that senior banker. I realized that what the lieutenant commander told me in Naval Leadership worked just as well at Morgan Stanley: "Praise in public, criticize in private."

How a leader criticizes or provides timely feedback is a key area of inspiration and engagement. Feedback is necessary and can be constructive if it is given in a balanced and professional manner.

You won't forget how your boss makes you feel if you feel that your boss is consistent, you can count on how the boss is going to react, your boss is generally enthusiastic about your accomplishments, your boss wants you to get ahead, and your boss acts like a coach. Consistency and support remove feelings of insecurity among team members and create emotional energy to put into the team's efforts.

You will not forget if you feel like the boss truly has your back. In my experience, a great leader creates a positive and supportive atmosphere on the team.

IMPORTANCE OF OPTIMISTIC LEADERSHIP

> "No pessimist ever discovered the secret of the stars, or sailed an unchartered land, or opened a new doorway for the human spirit."
>
> *Helen Keller, American author, political activist, and lecturer*

> "A pessimist sees the difficulty in every opportunity; an optimist the opportunity in every difficulty."
>
> *Winston Churchill, Prime Minister of the United Kingdom*

Another important factor in being an effective leader is to demonstrate optimism. In *The Leadership Advantage,* Warren Bennis wrote that optimism is one of the key things people need from their leaders in order to create engagement and achieve positive results. Every "exemplary leader that I have met," writes Bennis, "has what seems to be an unwarranted degree of optimism—and that helps generate positive results and commitment necessary to achieve results. The optimism in you will provide encouragement, strengthen engagement, and give your team the faith they need to achieve goals."

Highly effective leaders have a transforming effect on their constituents: they have the gift of being able to convince their followers that the team has the ability to achieve levels of performance beyond those it thought possible. While acknowledging reality, these leaders are able to paint an optimistic and attainable view of the future for their followers.

We naturally seek leaders who are optimists. We want leaders who will face obstacles head on, analyze them and formulate solutions, and then lead us around them. Optimists look for partial solutions, they avoid analysis paralysis, they are open to taking small steps toward achieving success. In General George Patton's military campaigns this pragmatic tactic was called "Bypass and Haul Ass," which means do not get bogged down trying to overcome every obstacle or objection that can prevent you and your team from making overall progress.

Nobel-prize-winning economist Daniel Kahneman discussed his research of optimists and their ability to lead others in the face of setbacks in his book, *Thinking Fast and Slow*. He said it's the resilience of optimists in the face of failure, their ability to adapt and rebound, that sets them apart from everybody else.

The optimism of a leader is contagious. The behavior of leaders and their attitudes will impact everyone around them, especially their followers. Your team must believe that no matter how bad things look, you will make them better. On several occasions I have been asked to rally our troops. I used a template that started by urging them to focus on controllables and by giving them several specific reasons to be upbeat. I provided credible context and perspective concerning bigger obstacles we had overcome in the past. I assured them the external buffeting we were currently facing would pass. I finished by saying why I believed in the company's strategy, its strong competitive position, and the quality of its talent. People told me these presentations were effective because I was authentic and convincing. You will want to develop your own outline for those times when your team needs optimism and encouragement to move forward and be engaged and achieve its potential.

DEFINITION OF A GOOD BOSS

"A leader is a dealer in hope."

Napoleon Bonaparte, French military and political leader

If you are the boss, what does your team want from you? They want you to provide them with the three *P*s: parameters, progress, and promotion. An effective leader will give each team member all three *P*s as seen in figure 18.1.

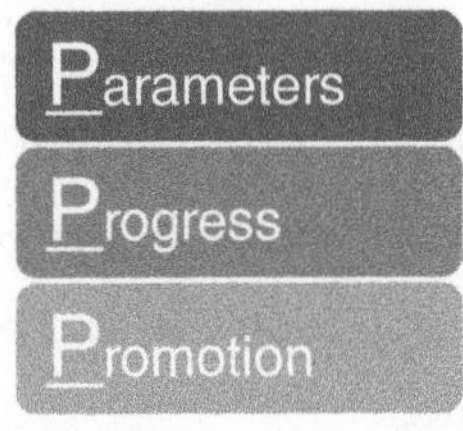

Figure 18.1 The Three *Ps*

Parameters

All employees need a clear understanding of the parameters of their job. When people are starting in a new career or a new role, they want to know "What is expected of me?" They do not necessarily need a written job description; they want a definition of their responsibilities or boundaries for what they are expected to do. They need to understand, "This is my job. This is what I should be focused on." Team members must understand their roles, what is expected of them, and how their efforts will be evaluated.

Progress

Team members want to grow in their career. They want to work with you and for you. They want you to give them the support, opportunities, training, and experiences to expand their skill set. They want more responsibility and more experience. They want a chance to step up and improve. An effective leader treats all team members with respect and has a sincere interest in their career growth as they progress in their new job.

As your employees master the parameters of their current job, you should identify opportunities that will allow them to grow their skill sets and motivate them to progress. An ideal boss helps each team member map a career growth plan and provides opportunities for each person to take on more. These new opportunities allow all team members to expand their capabilities and confidence.

These new opportunities could be increased exposure to clients, more responsibility on an engagement, an opportunity to lead a team. For example, if you take a team member to a client meeting, you should carve out a speaking role for that team member during the meeting to begin to build that person's credibility with the client. Then you should give that team member the role of following up with the client after the meeting. This is a vote of confidence in that team member from you in front of the client. Now the client will begin to think of your team member differently, and the team member has an opportunity to rise to the occasion.

A great boss lets a team member take a calculated career risk and will "take a bullet" for that team member if things do not work out. A bad boss lets a team member take a calculated career risk and points the finger at that team member if things do not work out. An outstanding leader provides a team member with public recognition of that person's achievements so the person ends up as the opposite of your firm's "best-kept secret." There is significant career upside for a team member when you tell others about your team member's good work.

A great boss could also connect team members to other people who could help them achieve their career aspirations. In contrast, a weak boss steals credit for a team member's work and keeps that team member hidden away.

People join great companies, and they quit bad bosses. People join great companies for macro reasons like the CEO, corporate brand, benefits, or culture. However, all of the progress that we have been talking about comes from the immediate boss or micro factors. Once people join a new company, many people underestimate the importance of a good boss. The CEO is too busy to help your team members move up in the organization. As the immediate boss, you are the most critical person in helping team members advance their careers.

Promotion

If a team member meets and exceeds the job performance requirements and has progressed in building the required skill sets, then that team member should reasonably expect a promotion. You should see that Parameters + Progress = Promotion.

That is what your team members want from you. It takes thought on your part: "I have to give them some definition about what they are expected to do. Then I have to make sure that they are getting opportunities to get better and be better. When they show me that they can do what we asked and exceed expectations, then I have to make sure that I keep them by promoting them."

The promotion can take different forms, including more responsibility, more resources, higher compensation, and possibly a bigger title. I have learned that leaders motivate and inspire people to perform at their best all the time. Exceptional leaders learn to do this in a way that maintains integrity and builds the firm's franchise.

KNEE-JERK REACTION

> "God, grant me the serenity to accept the things I cannot change, the courage to change the things I can, and the wisdom to know the difference."
>
> *Reinhold Niebuhr, American theologian*

Everyone knows about the iconic test a physician does by tapping a knee with a rubber hammer. The leg kicks out without the patient thinking about it. That is normal behavior in the doctor's office, but highly inadvisable in business situations.

Team members (and clients) take careful notice of how leaders react to adversity and stress. If a leader acts without thinking, that is usually an emotional reaction. The best leaders (and professionals) strive to *respond* rather than *react.*

For example, when faced with a setback or a piece of unexpected bad news, a smart leader might say, "I need to sleep on my response," or "I have to think about that," before responding. To paraphrase King Edward VIII, who said never miss a chance to sit down, I suggest you never miss an opportunity to pause. When you pause, you give yourself the chance to turn judgment into *discernment*, which is the ability to thoughtfully distinguish what is appropriate and best for the situation. Waiting a few hours to reply to an email will likely allow you to send a response that is more measured and calm and is an excellent example of the benefits of pausing.

In my career, giving a knee-jerk reaction without pausing sometimes made me look like a jerk.

You never know when someone will need to step up to lead in an unexpected, extenuating circumstance. Several years ago, I was invited by a client to go fishing with six other senior business executives. We were on a barge offshore near southern Louisiana. The barge, which had full kitchen facilities and sleeping quarters, was anchored near a barrier island in the Gulf of Mexico. We were fishing with three guides who used all-terrain vehicles to take us from one fishing spot to the next. At dusk on the final day of the trip, we were riding in the ATVs when a guide spotted three bales washed up on the beach. Each bale was a cube about two feet on each side and was very well wrapped in thick plastic.

The guide used his fishing knife to cut the plastic and I saw a white powder spill out. I had a hunch it was contraband rather than sugar or salt.

The head guide immediately took charge and calmly told us it was cocaine and that we would all go immediately back to the barge. He said he would call the local sheriff to get the police involved.

We were very concerned that the bales were under surveillance and were there to be picked up by bandits. We guessed the bad guys would be armed with something more powerful than our fishing rods. By the time we got to the barge, it was dark and all of us were getting very anxious about our safety. About 8 p.m., the sheriff radioed the barge to say his boat had broken down en-route and he needed to have his brother-in-law find him and use his boat to bring him to us. It seemed like an eternity before the sheriff finally came aboard our barge at 11:30 p.m.

The head guide put the bales on the boat with the sheriff and asked the sheriff to take full credit for finding the bale. He also asked that there be no mention of our barge or our identities. A few days later, the Associated Press reported that the parish sheriff had found three bales of cocaine washed up on a local beach that contained 30 bricks of high-purity cocaine worth over $25 million. We were not mentioned.

The head guide had shown excellent judgment and leadership as he calmly found a way to deal with the contraband and the local authorities and keep us safe.

ADAPTIVE LEADERSHIP

> "Change happens when the pain of holding on becomes greater than the fear of letting go."
>
> *Spencer Johnson, author of* Who Moved My Cheese?

In the first section of this book, we discussed EQ and the value of adaptability for people starting their careers. Leaders also need to be adaptable, especially in today's fast-paced, global business environment.

You might have heard the terms *creative destruction* or *disruptive technology*. Creative destruction is a term coined by Joseph Schumpeter in his 1942 work, *Capitalism, Socialism and Democracy*. It is a "process of industrial mutation that incessantly revolutionizes the economic structure from within, incessantly destroying the old one, incessantly creating a new one."[1] Harvard Business School professor Clayton M. Christensen coined the term *disruptive technology* in his 1997 best-selling book, *The Innovator's Dilemma.*[2] A disruptive technology is one that displaces an established technology and shakes up the industry or a groundbreaking product that creates a completely new industry.

The existence of creative destruction or technological disruption means that leaders no longer can simply set a plan and ask the team to execute it. Some academic and military writers discuss this dynamic atmosphere in the context of greater VUCA, short for *volatility*, *uncertainty*, *complexity*, and *ambiguity*. VUCA describes the situations marked by change and challenges:

- *Volatility:* The tendency to fluctuate quickly and sharply.
- *Uncertainty:* The presence of doubt created by the inability to analyze or predict.
- *Complexity:* The lack of order or simplicity compounded by intricacies and connections.
- *Ambiguity:* Something that has unclear intentions or meaning. It is not explicit and difficult to understand.

For military leaders, VUCA underscores the importance of strategic decision making, readiness planning, risk management, and situational problem solving.

In his book with A. G. Lafley, *Playing to Win: How Strategy Really Works*, Roger Martin defines strategy as making an integrated set of five choices that include "where to play" and "how to win."[3] This requires leaders to be attuned to the state of the economy and markets, regulation, competitors, and technology on a macro basis.

---

[1]Joseph A. Schumpeter, *Capitalism, Socialism and Democracy* (London: Routledge, 1994 [1942]), pp. 82–83. Retrieved November 23, 2011.
[2]Clayton M. Christensen, *The Innovator's Dilemma* (New York: Harper Business School Press).
[3]A. G. Lafley and Roger Martin, *Playing to Win: How Strategy Really Works* (Boston: Harvard Business Review Press, 2013), p. 5.

Adaptive leaders also can demonstrate their adjustments on a micro basis. For example, leaders can inspire their team members by being:

- Willing to try a different approach once in a while
- Willing to listen and consider a new idea before saying no
- First to try a new piece of hardware or software
- Flexible in dealing with team members' individual styles or work hours, communication methods, and/or quirky personalities

In a dynamic business environment, it is important for leaders to change and adapt.

XIX

CONTROL THE CONTROLLABLES

> "The most difficult thing is the decision to act, the rest is merely tenacity. The fears are paper tigers. You can do anything you decide to do. You can act to change and control your life; and the procedure, the process is its own reward."
>
> *Amelia Earhart, Aviation pioneer*

The most happy and well-adjusted people I know are self-disciplined. They make a habit of being focused, leading a healthy lifestyle, and being intellectually curious and enthusiastic. They know how to separate the urgent from the important. Self-discipline enables you to get things done and command the respect of others.

In his book, *The Checklist Manifesto—How to Get Things Right*, Dr. Atul Gawande describes how the disciplined use of a checklist reduced infections and other complications in his surgery practice.[1] He discusses how

[1] Atul Gawande, *The Checklist Manifesto—How to Get Things Right* (New York: Metropolitan Books, 2009).

by-the-book routine can be more important than intuition or individual infallibility. His book provides other examples of better outcomes for pilots and investors using disciplined procedures. This approach is especially relevant in the faster-paced environment that includes volatility and uncertainty.

Controllables include the goals or targets you set for the team, a schedule or timeline of deliverables against those goals, the costs and resources you invest, and the communication and teamwork you reinforce along the way. All of these controllables contribute to creating a durable business model and robust internal culture alongside the excellent client service you can deliver.

In sports, coaches often say, "You play like you practice." I have learned that you can control the process, but not the outcome. A strong process will not ensure results, but will certainly raise the probability of a desired outcome. Sound process and technique is the playbook of a successful team. This will give the team the clear objectives and priorities it is looking for. Differentiating between the controllable and the noncontrollable, combined with self-discipline and accountability, will enable you to direct your team's energy toward the controllable and allow team members to avoid wasting time and energy on those factors that are beyond their control. Consistent use of process will show the team the value of being systematic and data driven and will make you an exceptional leader and manager.

XX

CLOSING ADVICE

TEN BOOKS THAT MIGHT HELP YOU

"The more that you read, the more things you will know. The more that you learn, the more places you'll go."

Dr. Seuss, American writer and illustrator

1. *Kiss, Bow or Shake Hands* by Terri Morrison and Wayne A. Conaway. This book will help you avoid cultural faux pas in business and travel in more than 60 countries. It provides the basics of culture, history, and language for each country. You will learn what is expected when doing business in various countries, including tips for negotiating and decision making. You will also learn how to greet people in various cultures as well as what to wear.
2. *How to Say It* by Rosalie Maggio. This is a valuable guide and reference rather than a book to read. When you are staring at a blank screen or piece of stationery, use this book to quickly find words or phrases that allow you to custom tailor an email or message in your own voice. Written communication is a vital

soft skill in both your professional and personal life, and this book will improve your writing. The topics include thank-you notes, apologies, congratulations, condolences, and more.

3. *The Boys in the Boat: Nine Americans and Their Epic Quest for Gold at the 1936 Olympics* by Daniel James Brown. The inspiring story of the 1936 U.S. Olympic rowing team competing in the Berlin Olympics demonstrates that there is no limit to what a team can do when armed with determination and a positive attitude.
4. *The Ascent of Money* by Niall Ferguson. Well-known economic historian presents the development of money: the rise of currency and credit, and the histories of the bond market, the stock market, insurance, and the real-estate market as well as bubbles. He demonstrates the connection between money and human progress and describes how bankers play a vital role in capitalism.
5. *First 90 Days* by Michael D. Watkins. This is a guide to career transition periods when a new job or promotion puts you in a new role or you report to a new boss. You will find practical steps that managers can take in the first 90 days to learn the ropes and initiate changes. The author cautions managers not to assume that their existing skills will work well in their new roles and encourages them to pursue low-level, early wins to boost credibility while avoiding premature mistakes.
6. *How to Win Friends and Influence People* by Dale Carnegie. "It changed my life," said Warren Buffett. "The most successful self-help book of all time. . . . Carnegie has never seemed more relevant." Carnegie had a unique understanding of human nature. Career success, the author believed, is due 15 percent to professional knowledge and 85 percent to "the ability to express ideas, to assume leadership, and to arouse enthusiasm among people." Carnegie cautions against manipulating people and provides skills and techniques to make people feel genuinely important and appreciated.

7. *The Only Game in Town* by Mohamed El-Erian. Who knew a book on macroeconomics could be so enlightening, clear, and relevant? Slow global growth, rising inequality, high pockets of unemployment, and jumpy financial markets are leading the world to a fork in the road. The central banks can no longer be the "only game in town" to determine whether we take the path that leads to renewed growth, prosperity, and financial stability or the path to recession and market disorder. Households, investors, companies, and governments each have consequential choices to make in deciding our future direction.
8. *Who Moved My Cheese* by Spencer Johnson. Things change. Learn to adapt. This enlightening allegory illustrates the vital importance of being able to deal with the unexpected. The lessons it teaches can benefit anyone looking for less stress and more success in every aspect of work and life.
9. *Good to Great* by James C. Collins. There are no silver bullets that enable a good company to become great. Collins and his team of researchers examined 1,435 companies and found common traits among those companies that had made significant upward strides in performance. The authors found that these traits were unconventional in the context of prevailing wisdom about corporate success. They show that an overarching investment by everyone in the corporate culture trumps strategy, technology, or even a superstar CEO in making the transition from good to great.
10. *Outliers* by Malcolm Gladwell. This book says that once people score about 130, IQ becomes less important and intangibles become more important. Gladwell emphasizes intangibles such as a person's tenacity and agility. A key part of Gladwell's thesis is that how hard one works is essential to one's likelihood of success. Specifically, willingness to practice is a vital component of the accomplishments of the people Gladwell describes in this book.

HIGHLY PRACTICAL TIPS

- Meetings:
  - If you are able to pick the starting time, pick a time such as 10:15 a.m. rather than 10:00 a.m. Attendees will notice the precision and will usually show up on time.
  - Reconfirm all client meetings the day before, especially those involving travel.
  - If you agreed to meet but can no longer meet, use the word *postpone* rather than *cancel*. Postpone is less abrupt and shows you are still interested in getting together.
  - Arrive the night before for a morning client meeting. Clients are not amused if you miss the meeting because the morning plane was delayed or you missed your connection.
  - Ask colleagues to introduce themselves in a client meeting. This gives them a voice in the meeting. It allows them to pronounce their name correctly and properly describe their role and title.
  - If a client offers you a beverage at the beginning of a meeting, you should accept it. The client is really offering hospitality, and you can get off on the wrong foot by refusing. You don't have to finish the beverage.
  - Arrive early for internal meetings. You might be able to help a colleague who is running the meeting. You could chat with another person who also arrives early and get to know that person better. You will get a seat at the conference table and be able to effectively participate rather having to stand with those who arrive "fashionably late."
  - Former House speaker Carl Albert is reported to have said, "You can't beat something with nothing." What he meant was that it is useless to say, "That is a terrible idea" or "I am opposed to that." It is much more effective to say, "That is a poor choice, I have a better option and here is why." This method turns you from a naysayer into a constructive solution provider.

- Personal interactions:
  - A person's name is the greatest connection to their own identity and individuality. Using a person's name is crucial, especially when meeting people you have not seen in a while. Remembering a person's name and using it whenever appropriate indicates respect and recognition. When sending an email, make the extra effort to add a person's name to even the shortest message. For example, say "Thanks, Eli," or "Way to go, Kate."
  - When meeting someone who might not remember your name, say, "Hi, I'm Jim Runde. It's great to see you again." This ensures that the conversation gets off to a more comfortable start. It is a much better approach than saying, "Do you remember me?" or, "We met before."
  - When returning a missed phone call, say, "I am sorry I missed your call." This approach is more friendly than, "What's up?" or, "You called?"
  - A book is a great gift for colleagues or clients. Include a handwritten note that says, "You might find this of interest."
- Legendary lawyer Joe Flom once told me, "Always have the other guy work off your draft."
  - The document you draft could be an actual contract or engagement letter, but could also be a job description, a project description, or even an internal announcement about you that will be sent by your boss. Joe explained that missing the opportunity to produce a first draft happens because you do not have the interest or time. Creating a first draft often consumes substantially more resources than reviewing and editing someone else's draft. Taking the initiative and doing the hard work upfront means that the other person will work off your structure and will often just move around the semicolons and nip around the edges of your proposal, but the basic foundation of your proposal will remain intact. Hence,

the opportunity to voluntarily "grab the pen" and create the first draft can indeed be priceless. The best first draft should be clear and complete and balance your needs and wants without being so one sided as appearing to be overreaching or acting in bad faith.

- There will be times in your career where you face important issues that require a decision. Here is a suggested checklist for sorting things out:
  - Am I motivated by integrity, or am I being self-serving?
  - Am I striving for an excellent and practical work product or outcome, or am I striving for the perfect solution?
  - Am I being impulsive or decisive?
  - Am I deciding based on fear or anger?
  - What happens if I do nothing to address the issue right now?
  - I suggest you talk to someone in your network. Go through this list with them and ask if you are missing anything, review the pros and cons of your options, and discuss how you can avoid analysis paralysis. Also, you can use this checklist when you are acting as a mentor and someone asks you to help them think through an important decision.
- If you develop an active and responsible mindset, then you will empower yourself by:
  - Using your initiative, network, and resourcefulness to position yourself to make career choices rather than take career chances.
  - Actively honing and expanding your skills by reading and questioning and practicing rather than waiting for someone to spoon-feed you.
  - Hanging around with people who make you more positive and productive, rather than people who are dull or cynical.
  - Emphasizing persistence, which is active, rather than patience, which is passive.

SUMMARY

Banks and other professional services firms are facing a shortage of talent, especially talent with the right mindset, which means a proven ability to network, create trust-based client relationships, lead people, embrace the firm's strategy and culture, and deliver commercial results. My goal in this book is to help you to learn from my experience—and my mistakes—so that you can manifest the right talent with the right mindset at every stage of your career.

Early in your career, you probably discovered that you, like all your colleagues, are smart and hard working. Soft skills such as EQ (adaptability, collegiality, and empathy) are vital to distinguishing yourself at the beginning of your career. Understanding your firm's culture and incorporating it into your behavior is another key to getting ahead. Other important priorities include communicating with your boss, networking, and finding mentors and sponsors. All of these form the foundation for the magic formula of ability, opportunity, and courage.

When serving clients in the second phase of your career, trust and likability are more powerful than encyclopedic knowledge or knowing complex equations. It is important, but difficult, to build relationships and turn those relationships into revenue. You need to master the arts of creating insight out of information and using your time wisely.

The third career phase involves leading people and building teams. This book provides advice and examples of how to better engage and motivate team members and what makes a good boss. In today's business world, a leader needs to adapt to changes in technology, demographics, and volatility.

Now I encourage you to go out and apply these ideas and suggestions in the real world. The success of this book will be measured by how well this book changes your mindset and, more importantly, your behavior. I hope I have given you some tools that will help you build a satisfying and successful career.

ABOUT THE AUTHOR

James A. Runde is a trusted adviser to a number of the world's leading companies, both as an investment banker and as an independent corporate director. He is the longest-serving investment banker at a single U.S. firm, having spent over 40 years at Morgan Stanley. Jim is a director of the Kroger Company, the large national grocery chain, and previously served as a director of Burlington Resources, a large exploration and production company. He is also a trustee of the Morgan Library and Marquette University.

Jim grew up in Sparta, Wisconsin. He was awarded a scholarship from the Naval Reserve Officer Training Corps and pursued an electrical engineering degree from Marquette University in Milwaukee. Jim served as an officer in the U.S. Navy for five years while also earning a master's degree in finance from George Washington University School of Business.

Jim is well known for his role advising UPS on its famous and difficult decision to go public. He is widely recognized for his transportation and infrastructure expertise, and has testified before Congress.

Within Morgan Stanley, Jim's skills as a banker became legendary, as it became apparent that Jim was equally effective in the technology and energy sectors as he was in transportation. Jim was appointed vice chairman. In addition to his client-facing roles, Jim was asked if he could educate other bankers about emotional intelligence quotient (EQ), trust-based client relationships, and other soft skills. It wasn't long before

Jim's presentations went global, became oversubscribed, and were sought out by professional services firms as well.

This book was created based on Jim's presentations. His parents were both schoolteachers and passed on to him the valuable role of coaching and mentoring as important life skills. Readers will find many practical tips and tools to improve their performance at all levels of their careers.

INDEX

Page references followed by "f" indicate a figure and "t" indicate table.

A

Ability, impact, 51
Achievement, impact, 126
Adaptability, 6–7
Adaptability
 Collegiality/collaboration
 Empathy (ACE), 6–11
Adaptive leadership, 134–136
Adversity
 adaptation, 7–8
  ability, 8
 leader reaction, 133
Agassi, Andre, 42
Alacrity, 17–18
Ali, Muhammad, 38
Ambiguity, 135
Appearance, enhancement, 46
Apple Store, 89
Approach Probe Present Listen End
 (APPLE) steps, usage, 89–90
Arrogance (promotion factor), 24
Arthur Young, 98
Ascent of Money,
 The (Ferguson), 140
Assignment, completion, 18
Assistant, relationship, 76–77
Association of Graduate
 Recruiters, 57
Assurance, provision, 11
Authority, 73
Awareness, requirement, 38

B

Bake-off, 63, 92
Balance-of-trade conversations,
 93–94
Bear Stearns, 98
Beauty contest, 63–64
Bennis, Warren, 128
Berra, Yogi, 30
Bezos, Jeff, 112
Bidding, example, 101–102
Bonaparte, Napoleon, 130
Books, usage, 139–141
Boss
 cup of coffee, sharing, 26–27
 employees, relationship, 35
 good boss, definition, 130–132
 interaction, 114
 lifestyle/geography/pay, 36f
 parameters, 130
 progress, 130–132
 promotion, 132
Boys in the Boat, The (Brown), 140
Brafman, Ori/Rom, 79
Brains, 3
 indication, 24

Brands
  creation process, 98
  premium brand, 97–98
  strength, 98
  value, 97
Breindel, DeSantis, 98
Brown, Daniel James, 140
Brown, Paul B., 63
Buffett, Warren, 97
Building, 98
Business
  changes, 105–106
  etiquette, 47
  improvement, 97
  repeat business, benefits, 69
  strategy, amalgamation, 98
  winning, process, 63

C

Capitalism, Socialism and Democracy (Schumpeter), 134
Career
  development, 14
  growth, employer provision, 119
  headwinds/tailwinds, navigation, 39–40
  initiation, 9
  issues, 144
  order, steps, 60f
  risk, 38
    taking/calculating, 109
  roadmap, creation, 38
  setback, suffering, 40
Carnegie, Dale, 140
Checklist Manifesto, The (Gawande), 137
Chemistry, consideration, 111
Chief executive officers (CEOs), talent (questions), 117
Christensen, Clayton M., 135
Churchill, Winston, 52, 128
Cialdini, Robert, 72, 73
Click (Brafman), 79
Client-centered relationship model, 69, 69f
Client Relationship Diagram, 69f
Client relationships, 60
  building, 67–68
    flowchart, 67f
  diagram, 70f
  long-term client-centered approach, 81
  long-term client relationship, 58
    building, objective, 93
  loyalty, 67, 87
  maintenance, 71–72
  monetization, process, 69–72
  revenue generation, 58–59
  trust-based client relationships, 100–102
Clients
  CFO, joining, 6–7
  competitors, identification, 91
  coverage, 93
  differentiation, 87–88
  empathy, 11
  engagement, execution, 96–97
  exposure, increase, 131
  future revenue, knowledge, 91–92
  importance, 124
  interaction, 82–83
  interests, placement, 85–86
  loyalty, erosion, 97–98
  meeting, preparation process, 75, 76f
  negotiation, 71–72
  personal relationships, leverage, 99
  progress, knowledge, 92–94

rejection, avoidance, 83–84
self-differentiation, 85–89
service business, long-term success, 60
situation, assessment, 91
technology, preparation, 16
trust
building, 10
impact, 11
vital signs, knowledge, 91–92
Close, usage, 79–81
Co-creation, employee goal, 121
Collaboration, 8–9
importance, 8
Collegiality, importance, 124
Collins, James C., 141
Comfort, provision, 11
Command-and control management, 108
Commercial appeal, increase, 59–62
Commercial awareness, 57–58
Commercial impact, firm strategy (connection), 96–97, 96f
Commercial instinct (promotion factor), 25
Commercial relevance, importance, 57
Commitment/consistency, 72
Communication
clarity, 110
differentiator, 109
proactive cross-cultural communication, creation, 122
problem, 24
promotion factor, 25
skills, 46
usage, 110, 138
Compensation, 37
Competitive advantage, sustaining, 119
Competitors
identification, 91
truth, economy, 66
Complexity, 135
Compliment, impact, 127–128
Composition, 111
Composition Chemistry Continuity (3*C*s), 111–112
Conaway, Wayne A., 139
Confidence
self-confidence, building, 114
vote, 131
Confucius, 75
Congratulatory emails, response rate, 33
Controllables, 137–138
noncontrollable, differentiation, 138
Cooperative spots, 77
Corporate culture, importance, 40
Corporate IPO, 66
Corporate ladder, moving, 6–7
Corporate mobility, management, 36
Cotton, Gayle, 122
Courage, impact, 52–53
Couric, Katie, 42
Coverage team, 93–94
Covey, Stephen M.R., 100
Co-workers, interaction, 114
Creative destruction, 134–135
existence, 135
Credibility, restoration, 95
Cross-cultural communication, creation, 122
Cultural beliefs, understanding, 123

Cultural gap (bridging), rapport (establishment), 122
Culturally sensitive interaction, management, 86
Culture, 39, 118
  clients, importance, 124
  differences, 122, 123–124
Currency, 33–34
Customers, interaction, 114

D

Darwin, Charles, 6
Data, correctness, 19–21
Davis Polk and Wardwell, xi
Day job, 109
  role, 110–111
Deadlines, knowledge, 17–19
Deal, closure, 68
Decisions
  balance, 46
  requirement, 144
Deep-subject-matter expert, 108
Deliverables
  expectations, 18
  location, 17–18
  overlap, 18
Dell, Michael, 42
Deloitte Millennial Survey, 119–120
Demographic turnover/variations, 121
Demographic turnover/variations, Digital and mobile, Different markets/cultures (3*D*s), 121–123
Details
  attention, 20
  importance, 15–17
  roadblocks, 16
Details Deadlines Data (3*D*s), 13
Dewey and LeBouef, 98
Differentiation, component, 97
Digital revolution, transformation, 121–122
Discernment, judgment conversion, 133
Discontinuity, impact, 112
Disraeli, Benjamin, 7
Disruptive technology, 134–135
Dissatisfaction, factors (Herzberg), 126t
Distractions, elimination, 32
Diversity, 119
Document, drafting, 143–144
Draft, usage, 143–144
Dream job, roadmap (creation), 38–39
Dysfunctional workers, handling (difficulty), 112

E

Edward VIII, 133
El-Erian, Mohamed, 141
Elevator pitch, 41–42
Ellis, Charles, 123
Emotional hardships, 11
Emotional Intelligence (Goleman), 5
Emotional intelligence quotient (EQ), 3
Emotional quotient (EQ), 5
  IQ, comparison, 4
  relationships, comparison, 5
  usage, 51
Empathy, 9–11
  importance, 11
  sympathy, contrast, 11
Employees
  co-creation, goal, 121
  interviews, 113
  retention strategies, 118–119
Employment opportunities, 52

Encyclopedia, trusted adviser (contrast), 25
Engagement, 118
  responsibility, increase, 131
Epictetus, 10
Ethics (promotion factor), 25
Evaluations, 23
Exceptional leadership, importance, 125
Exceptional service, 100–101
Execution-oriented professionals, 60
Expectations, 23
  transparency, 120
Experience, increase, 130
Eye contact, 32
  avoidance, 41

F

Farley, Mike, 48
Feedback, necessity/importance, 128
Fee negotiation, 70
Ferguson, Niall, 140
Ferrazzi, Keith, 30
Financial constraint, 117
finviz.com, usage, 33
Firms
  best-kept secret, 131
  client hiring, 97–99
  culture, 118
  long-term good, 25
  strategy, 118
    commercial basis, 95
    commercial impact, connection, 96–97, 96f
    knowledge, 95–96
  words, usage, 98–99
First 90 Days (Watkins), 140
Fisher, Roger, 70
Flom, Joe, 143
Focus, demonstration, 65
Followership, leadership (comparison), 110
Ford, Henry, 111

G

Gates, Bill, 42
Gawande, Atul, 137
Gen Xers, motivation, 120
Geographic preference, 36
Getting to Yes (Fisher/Ury/Patton), 70
Gilbert, Parker, xv
Gladwell, Malcolm, 141
Goldsmith, Marshall, 7, 107
Goleman, Daniel, 5
Good boss, definition, 130–132
Good to Great (Collins), 141
Gorman, James, xv
Greenspan, Alan, 42
Group success, 111
Growth, driving, 119

H

Happiness, improvement, 37–38, 126
Hard work, 3
Herzberg, Frederick, 125, 126
Hiring, avoidance, 112
Holmes, Sr., Oliver Wendell, 87
Hopper, Grace, 105
Howard, Ron, 42
How to Say It (Maggio), 139–140
How to Win Friends and Influence People (Carnegie), 140

I

Impression, making, 42–43
Inclusiveness (promotion factor), 24

Individual infallibility,
importance, 138
Influence, principles, 72–73
Information, insight
conversion, 88
Innovation, 119
impact, 118
Innovator's Dilemma, The
(Christensen), 135
Insights, usage, 76
Integrity, 110
importance, 124
Intellect, importance, 106
Intelligence quotient (IQ)
EQ, comparison, 4
filtering, 24
Interactions, organization, 122
Internal mobility, employer
provision, 119
Internal preparation
meetings, 43
Interview, 114
questions, 113
Interviewee
job experience, 113
skills, 114
Intuition, importance, 138

J

Job
candidate pool, 118
dissatisfaction, 125–126
factors, 126
happiness, improvement, 126
hoppers, 39
parameters, mastery, 131
responsibilities, 108–111
search, 114
Johnson, Spencer, 134, 141
Judgment
conversion, 133
promotion factor, 24
Junior people, treatment
(promotion factor), 25

K

Kahneman, Daniel, 129
Kelleher, Colm, xv
Keller, Helen, 128
Kiss, Bow or Shake Hands
(Morrison/Conaway), 139
Knee-jerk reaction, 132–134
Know (magic word), 100
Knowledge, development, 46
Krzyzewski, Mike, 82

L

Lafley, A.G., 135
Leaders
adversity/stress reaction, 133
awareness, 135
criticism, impact, 128
differentiator, 109
managers, comparison, 106
optimism, 129
roles, 110–111
skill/adaptability, 121–123
transforming effects, 129
Leadership, 108–111
adaptive leadership, 134–136
exceptional leadership,
importance, 125
followership, comparison, 110
job, 109
optimistic leadership,
importance, 128–129
promotion factor, 25
responsibilities, increase,
107–108
Leadership Advantage, The
(Bennis), 128
Lehman Brothers, 98

Lifestyle, 35–36
geography/pay, 36f
Likability, usage, 85–87
Like (magic word), 100
Liking, 73
Lives, enriching, 89
Lombardi, Vince, 8
Lone wolf, team player (contrast), 25
Long-term client-centered relationship, 81
Long-term client relationship, 58
building, objective, 93
creation, 69
maintenance, 71, 72
Loyalty, building, 89

M

Maggio, Rosalie, 139
Management
ability, 108–111
job, 109
Managers
leaders, comparison, 106
roles, 110–111
Mandela, Nelson, 72
Markets, differences, 122
Market share, gaining, 95
Marquette University, 4, 147
Martin, Roger, 135
Mays, Willie, 42
McCartney, Paul, 42
Meaning, 120–121
Meetings, 32, 89
advice, 142
internal preparation meetings, 43
seating arrangements, 77
summarization, 101
Memorandum, preparation, 19–20
Mentors, 37, 46–48
assistance, absence, 52–53
characteristics, 47
choice, 47
sponsors, comparison, 48
Mentorship, 120
Mergers-and-acquisitions (M&A), 92
Meritocracy Mentorship Meaning (3*M*s), 119–121
Metrics, 39, 40
Millennials, motivation, 120
Mindset, 118
change, 78–79
development, 144
Mobile challenges, 121–122
Mobility, 119
corporate mobility, management, 36
internal mobility, employer provision, 119
Money, importance, 36–37
Morrison, Terri, 139
Motivation-Hygiene Theory (Herzberg), 125–126
Multi-cultural interactions, organizing, 122

N

Negotiation, process, 70
Networking, 39, 47
activity, 31
benefits, 29, 31
currency, 33–34
fork, 30f
icebreakers, 32–33
risks, 29
selection, 30
systematic approach, 31–32

Networks
development, importance, 31
strength, 40
Never Eat Alone (Ferrazzi/Raz), 303
Niebuhr, Reinhold, 132
Noncontrollable, controllables (differentiation), 138

O

Objections
anticipation, 83
categories, 83
Odyssey, The, 47
Only Game in Town, The (El-Erian), 141
Open-ended questions, asking, 79–80
Opening close, usage, 79–81
Openness, trust relationship (building), 10
Opportunity
constraint, 117
impact, 52
Optimism
mindset, development, 7–8
usage, 110
Optimistic leadership, importance, 128–129
Order
asking, process, 81–82
steps, 60f
Organization
corporate culture, 40
perception, 35
Organizational culture, manifestation, 123
Organizational success, 95
Outcomes, 77–78
examples, 137–138
Outer circle, 72
Outliers (Gladwell), 141

P

Parameters
equation, 132
mastery, 52
Parameters Progress Promotion (3*P*s), 130–132, 130f
Part-time job, holding, 113–114
Patton, Bruce, 70
Patton, George, 129
Paulson, Henry, 42
Pay, analysis, 36–37
People
duty/obligation, 73
engaging/leading, 105
exposure, 14
knowledge, number (increase), 29
meeting, initiation, 32
selection, 106–107
Perception, importance, 67
Performance evaluation
criteria, knowledge, 23, 40
forms, differences, 107
Performance measurement, 120
Perot, Ross, 100
Persistence, habit, 7–8
Personal connection, 100–101
Personal interactions, advice, 143
Personal responsibility, 113–114
Persuasion, process, 70
improvement, 72–73
Peter, Laurence J., 106
Peter Principle, 106–107
Pitch, 63–64
book, updating, 65–66
team checklist, 65
tone, 64–65
Pitch time allocations, 64t
Playing to Win (Lafley/Martin), 135

Play, practice (comparison), 138
Positive attitude
  maintenance, 15
  usefulness, 14
Practice, play (comparison), 138
Premium brand, 97–98
Presentation
  delegation, 65–66
  skills, 47
Principles of influence, 72–73
Private-sector workforce,
    evolution, 108–109
Proactive cross-cultural
    communication,
    creation, 122
Problem solving, 57
Productive interactions,
    organization, 122
Productivity
  generation, 95
  impact, 118
Professional identity, creation, 14
Professional services, technical
    aspects, 59–60
Profit generation, 97
Progress, 130–132
  equation, 132
Projects
  completion, 68
  management, 18
Promotion, 24–25, 130f, 132
  decisions, 24, 48
  discussions, factors, 24–25
  equation, 132
Prucha, Paul, 48

Q

Quantitative analysis, checking, 20

R

Rapport, establishment, 122
Raz, Tahl, 30
Reaching, 75–76
Read Reach Raise Ready (4*R*s),
    75–78
Reagan, Ronald, 42
Reciprocation, 72
Reciprocity, importance, 33
Recognition, impact, 126
Recruitment, 118
Reiter, Mark, 107
Rejection, reactions, 82–83
Relationships
  building, strategies
    (pursuit), 123
  EQ, comparison, 5
  solidity, 17
Repeat business, benefits, 69
Reputation, expansion, 63–64
Request for proposals (RFPs), 63,
    65, 98
Reserve Officers Training Corps
    (ROTC) program, 127
Resilience
  characteristics (APA), 7
  development, 8
  promotion factor, 25
Responsibility
  impact, 126
  increase, 130
Retention, 118–119
Revenue generation, 58–59
Revenue growth, driving, 95
Rickover, Hyman G., 4, 58
Role models, 45–46
  addition, 45
  advice, provision, 46
  passivity, 46–47
Roosevelt, Franklin D., 108
Rotation philosophy, 92
Rules, understanding, 123

S
Sampras, Pete, 42
Satisfaction, factors
    (Herzberg), 126t
Sawyer, Diane, 42
Say Anything to Anyone, Anywhere
    (Cotton), 122
Scarcity, 73
Schumpeter, Joseph, 134
Screening, 112–116
  questions, 114
Seating arrangements, 77
Self-analysis, 35
Self-awareness, 6, 69, 70
Self-confidence, building, 114
Self-differentiation, 85–89
  insight, usage, 87–89
Self-discipline, impact, 137
Self-empowerment, 144
Self-promotion, 41
Selling, process, 70–71
Service
  Apple Five Steps, usage, 89–90
  exceptional service, 100–101
  professional services, 9
Services firms
  IQ, filtration, 24
  words, usage, 98–99
Seuss, Dr., 139
Sexton, Griff, xv
Sights, raising, 76
Skills
  development, 46
  shortages, 58t
Social capital, 29
Social proof, 72–73
Sparta, Wisconsin, 4, 147
Speaker, eye contact, 32
Speaking up, 42–43
Sponsors, 48–49
  mentors, comparison, 48
Sponsorship
  path, 45
  pyramid, 46f
Stress, leader reaction, 133
Success
  ability, 51
  clues, recognition, 123
  courage, impact, 52–53
  dressing, 47
  magic formula, 51
  opportunity, 52
  organizational success, 95
Summer jobs, character
    traits, 114
Surowiecki, James, 8
Swindoll, Charles R., 13
Sympathy, empathy (contrast), 11

T
Talent, 97, 120f
  constraints, 117
  holistic approach, 118–119
  issues, 121–123
  shortage, 118
  war, 117
Task, initiation, 15–16
Team
  ability, leaders (impact),
    128–129
  building, 3*C*s, 111–112
  caucus, requirement, 102
  checklist, 65
  client preference, 99
  continuity, 112
  coverage team, 93–94
  feelings, 127–128
  leaders, interview questions, 113
  leading, opportunity, 131
  motivation/engagement, 126
  player, lone wolf (contrast), 25

Team members, 112
  impact, 110
  organizational advancement, 131–132
  role, understanding, 130
  screening, 112–116
Teamwork, 57
  problem, 24
  usage, 138
Technological disruption, existence, 135
Technology, preparation, 16
Thinking Fast and Slow (Kahneman), 129
Third party, paychecks, 114
Thoughts, articulation (practice), 43
Ticker tape, 87–88
Treasurer, gatekeeper, 76
Trust, 73, 102
  magic word, 100
  openness, relationship (building), 10
  problem, 24
  restoration, 95
  usage, 85–87
Trust-based client relationships, 100–102
Trusted adviser, 68
  encyclopedia, contrast, 25
Truth, economy, 66
Twain, Mark, 31
Two-Factor Theory (Herzberg), 125
Tzu, Lao, 123

U

Uncertainty, 135
Unexpressed wishes/concerns, 89
Ury, William, 70

V

Value
  delivery, 93
  demonstration, 65
Values, 123–124
Volatility Uncertainty Complexity Ambiguity (VUCA), 135–136
von Goethe, Johann Wolfgang, 127
Vulnerability, display, 53

W

Walton, Sam, 127
Watkins, Michael D., 140
We/they dynamic, 77–78
What Got You Here Won't Get You There (Goldsmith), 7, 107
What It Takes (Ellis), 123
Whittier, John Greenleaf, 51
Who Moved My Cheese (Johnson), 141
Wilde, Oscar, 17
Willingness, requirement, 38
Wisdom of Crowds, The (Surowiecki), 8
Work
  basis, 106
  digital revolution, impact, 121–122
Workforce
  demographic turnover/variations, 121
  private-sector workforce, evolution, 108–109
Workplace
  experience, 114
  needs/wishes (3*M*s), 119–121